GREAT BRITISH STREET NAMES

From the Downright Weird to
the Simply Wonderful

CHRISTOPHER WINN

Hardie Grant

QUADRILLE

For Ann, 20 years of fun and friendship

Publishing Director Sarah Lavelle
Editorial Assistant Sofie Shearman
Copy Editor Kate Parker
Head of Design Claire Rochford
Cover Design Jack Smyth
Typesetter Vanessa Green
Head of Production Stephen Lang
Production Controller Sabeena Atchia

Published in 2021 by Quadrille, an imprint
of Hardie Grant Publishing

Quadrille
52-54 Southwark Street
London SE1 1UN
quadrille.com

Cataloguing in Publication Data: a
catalogue record for this book is available
from the British Library.

Text © Christopher Winn 2021
Design © Quadrille 2021

ISBN 978 1 78713 759 2
Printed in China

MIX
Paper from
responsible sources
FSC™ C020056

CONTENTS

PREFACE

What's in a street name? That which we call a street by any other name would still be a street. Or would it?

There are some 800,000 streets in England, Scotland and Wales that have a name, along with several thousand more in Northern Ireland. These names range from **Aachen Way** in Halifax to **Zurich Gardens** in Bramhall in Stockport. The longest street name in Britain is **Bolderwood Arboretum Ornamental Drive** in the New Forest in Hampshire. The shortest is **Rye**, in Puriton in Somerset.

There are more than 5,400 **High Streets**, but there is only one **Christmas Pie Avenue**. There are thousands of **Roads** and **Closes**, but very few **Vennels** and **Boulevards**. Some street names state the obvious - **Station Approach** or **River View**, for instance. Some are more obscure, like **Gillygate** or **Titty Ho**.

All of them tell you something - not just about where you are, but about the age, history, culture, geography, wealth, professions, preoccupations and people of where you are. And they can affect the price of your house, too. You are far more likely to get a good price for a house on **Parkview Avenue** or **Cherry Tree Lane** than on **Gas Works Road** or **Bog End**.

But beware. Once you start noticing street names, there's no going back. They are truly addictive.

So let *Great British Street Names* be your guide to a whole new world of fun, fascination and facts. Know where you are going. Learn how to work out the meaning of the most baffling names. Impress your friends. And by the time you have finished the book, you will have discovered a whole lot of new information about Britain.

INTRODUCTION

First of all, why do we need street names? Basically, they tell us where we are or how to find where we want to go. They identify and describe a location. As part of an address, they help us pinpoint an exact spot. They are essential so that the emergency services, police, Post Office and any individual can find and reference a property or amenity.

And once we accept the need for street names, how and why do we choose particular street names?

The final decision on what to name a new street rests with the local authority, but that decision is usually made in consultation with various others: the developers, local history groups, the Post Office, local councillors and residents. To change the name of an existing street, the local authority must have the consent of the property owners on the street under discussion.

But let's pause for a moment. Before we dive too far into the weird and wonderful world of street names, perhaps we should take a moment to ascertain what, actually, is a street?

According to my edition of the *Concise Oxford English Dictionary*, a street is a 'town or village road that has (mainly) contiguous houses on one or both sides'. So a street is in fact a specific type of road, 'road' being the general term we now use for any kind of line of communication on land used for moving from one place to another, be it a dirt track, a lane, a highway or an alleyway.

Why do we tend to use the term 'street names' rather than 'road names'? Well, to begin with, the word 'street' has been around much longer than the word 'road', as we will learn in the next chapter. The City of London, for instance, has no roads because its streets were named before 'roads' actually existed.

The word 'street' comes from the Latin *strata*, or more precisely *via strata* ('paved way'), derived in turn from *stratum*, which refers to something spread out or laid down (and also giving us 'stratum' in the sense of a layer). When the Romans invaded Britain, they laid down *stratae*, or paved roads, to enable their legions to move around the country efficiently. And once the Romans had gone, the Anglo-Saxons who replaced them - not great road builders themselves - continued to use the paved roads that the Romans had so thoughtfully constructed for them as major highways. Thus they applied the Latin-derived term 'street' to any paved road, in effect Roman roads, to distinguish them from the untreated muddy tracks that made up most of the everyday byways.

While recent excavations in Shropshire have uncovered evidence of paved roads built by Iron Age Britons, these were not long-lasting and would have mostly disappeared or become unusable before the Saxons arrived. So, the first Great British streets were, in fact, Roman roads. Indeed, the most important Roman roads in Britain are still called 'streets' today: **Ermine Street** from London to York; **Watling Street** from Dover to Chester; **Stane Street** from London to Chichester; and **Dere Street** from London to Cirencester.

When urbanisation began in earnest in the eighteenth century, the new roads tended to be paved, whereas those in the country remained untreated. The term 'street' thus applied more to paved urban streets than to unpaved country roads. In this way, a street became a type of road rather than a generic term, although the words 'street' and 'road' are still interchangeable in the public mind. And, as there are many more urban streets than rural roads, we tend to think of 'street names' first and use this as our given term, rather than 'road names'. Also, while the term 'street' is used for a specific thoroughfare that needs to be identified and therefore named, the term 'road', while it *may* be used for a specific thoroughfare, can also be used to describe thoroughfares in general. In other words, there are no unnamed streets but there are plenty of unnamed roads.

A major difference between a street and a road is that a street must be a public highway whereas a road can be private - there are many private roads but no private streets. In the eleventh century, English law, as laid out by the Anglo-Saxon King Edward the Confessor in his *Leges Edwardi Confessoris*, decreed that the four main surviving Roman roads or streets in Britain should be protected as public rights of way, and ever since then streets have been protected as public highways.

The way we use the terms 'street' or 'road' in everyday language helps to illustrate the difference. Expressions that use the word 'road' - 'road trip', 'road rage', 'middle of the road', 'rules of the road', 'one for the road', 'road works', 'roadshow', 'fork in the road' - tend to be more general in meaning. Those using 'street', by contrast - 'streetwise', 'street corner', 'city streets', 'the man on the street', 'one-way street', 'street theatre', 'street gangs', 'Civvy Street', 'Easy Street' - refer to pursuits or situations that are more specifically urban. Interestingly, there are no actual Civvy Streets or Easy Streets in Britain, but there is an **Easy Road**, in Leeds. And an **Easy Lane** in Rugby. Also, thank goodness, there is an **Easy Way**, in Luton. Who'd have thought?

Anyway, I hope this helps to explain why we give 'street' names to different kinds of road. So let's move on and examine how these names came about.

1

TYPES OF STREET

A street name is known as a hodonym, from the ancient Greek *hodos* - meaning 'journey', 'the action of travelling' or 'the way along which you travel' - and *onoma*, meaning 'name'. Hence 'the name of the way along which you travel'. Hodonyms are usually made up of two parts: the specific, which is the individual name of the street; and the generic, which indicates the type of street. In Northumberland Avenue, for example, 'Northumberland' would be the specific and 'Avenue' the generic. A more commonly used term for the generic part of a street name is 'suffix'. In fact, a street name is not unlike a person's name - it has a family name (Winn), which is the suffix and indicates which category of streets it belongs to, and an individual first name (Christopher), which acts as the specific.

For the moment we will concentrate on the suffix. Streets come in all different types and varieties, shapes and sizes, from motorways and major through roads with several lanes, to winding, single-carriageway back roads and side roads, to residential streets and avenues, to cul de sacs and narrow alleys and passageways. The particular nature of a street can be determined by the descriptive word or suffix that follows the name - Lane, Road, Crescent, Avenue and so on. In my ramblings around the country I have come across over eighty different suffixes - many of which mean much the same thing.

There are five categories of street suffix: major roads; small roads; roads named for their shape; roads named for geographical features or attributes; and those named for their function or purpose. You will notice that I use both 'street' and 'road'. This is because the terms are interchangeable when describing thoroughfares in general. But there is a subtle difference, which we will come to. For now, I will use whichever feels most appropriate depending on general usage. Hence 'major roads' feels right, 'major streets' does not.

Here is what the various suffixes mean, along with some examples, starting with major roads. Definitions come from the *Concise Oxford English Dictionary* (sixth edition).

MAJOR ROADS

The Saxons, from whom we inherit our earliest street names, had various terms for different kinds of thoroughfare. The generic term in Old English was *weg*, derived from an earlier sense of 'to move, carry' to mean a road, path or way. *Strata*, or 'street', as we have heard, which could also be rendered *straet* or *strate*, was used for a paved way, usually a Roman road. The modern 'lane' is taken straight from the Old English or Anglo-Saxon word *lane* or *lanu*, meaning a narrow way between hedges. 'Avenue', a way of approach and 'road', a way along which you can ride, didn't come along until much later.

WAY

A 'road, track, path provided for passing along', as in right of way, a means of access. 'Highway' refers in general terms to any type of public road, as in 'the public highway'. As a suffix, Way tends to be used for very ancient roads or, with increasing frequency, for small side streets. Way can also mean the best route between two points or the route generally taken by an important or historical figure or group of people, such as Canons Way or Abbots Way. Britain's most common Way is Kingsway or King's Way. There are close to three hundred Kingsways and quite a few Queensways, and they are invariably named in honour of the king or queen on the throne either when they were opened, or who opened them.

* **Kingsway** in London, although planned during the reign of Queen Victoria, was not completed until 1905 when it was opened by

Edward VII and named in his honour. London's **Queensway** was named after Queen Victoria as this was the way by which, as a princess, she rode out from Kensington Palace.

* **Pilgrims' Way**. There are up to a hundred Pilgrims' Ways in Britain, along which pilgrims would have travelled to various places of pilgrimage around the country, such as holy wells, religious sites or burial places. The most famous Pilgrims' Way is the Stone Age track that follows the natural east-west causeway along the top of the North Downs, and which was used by the pilgrims in Chaucer's *Canterbury Tales* on their journey from Winchester to Thomas Becket's tomb in Canterbury Cathedral. There is a **Pilgrim Street** in Newcastle upon Tyne that was the main way for pilgrims visiting the chapel of St Mary in Jesmond, as well as part of the Great North Road between Durham and the holy island of Lindisfarne.

STREET

A 'town or village road that has (mainly) contiguous houses on one or both sides'. As we have already seen, when most of the roads in Britain were simple unmade tracks, the term 'street' referred to any paved road, or in effect Roman roads. Very often there was only one paved road running through a community and this would be referred to as **The Street**. There are some three hundred roads in Britain bearing this name, and you can be pretty sure that they are all old and most likely follow the route of a Roman road. There is only one street I have been able to find called simply **Street**, just outside the Cumbrian village of Great Strickland, and it is, indeed, a one and a quarter mile section of straight road that follows the route of a Roman road.

A good example is The Street in Rickinghall in Suffolk, the old coaching road between Norwich and Bury St Edmunds. It is a long, straight road lined with Tudor cottages and ancient inns, which follows the line of an old Roman road and runs through the centre of three villages, Rickinghall Superior, Rickinghall Inferior and Botesdale. Rickinghall was the home of Basil Brown, the archaeologist who excavated the Anglo-Saxon ship burial at Sutton Hoo in 1939. A street in the village has been named **Basil Brown Close** in his honour.

Some time around the twelfth century, the word 'high' began to be applied to The Street, 'high' coming from the Anglo-Saxon *heah*, meaning 'lofty', 'elevated' or 'exalted' (as in 'high sheriff' or 'high society') and thus indicating that the High Street was the most important street in the village. Today **High Street** is by some margin Britain's most common street name since virtually every community - almost by definition - has one. There are something over 3,000 High Streets and another 2,000 or more streets with variations on the name, such as **Upper High Street** or **High Street North**.

The ever-practical Scots tend to call their main street, er, **Main Street**, and Main Street is thus the most common street name in Scotland.

As towns and cities expanded rapidly in Georgian and Victorian times, so the number of High Streets multiplied, and since shops and commercial enterprises tended to cluster along the main street of any community, the term High Street became more generic and applied to any area where the main shops were clustered ('the high street') and to national shop chains ('high-street shops').

ROAD

A 'line of communication, specially prepared track between places for use of pedestrians, riders and vehicles'. The word 'road' comes from the Old English word *ridan*, meaning 'to ride', and 'road' thus originally referred to any track or way that you could ride along. It then became the most widely used term for describing any kind of thoroughfare, hence Road is now the most common suffix. Once the Industrial Revolution brought about the expansion of towns and cities, leading to more and more paved roads (streets) being built, there was no longer any meaningful distinction between a road and a street. 'Road' came to refer to any paved thoroughfare or line of communication with a stabilised base, such as a gravel road, be it in the town or in the country, while streets evolved into urbanised roads with buildings running alongside.

The most common name for a road, and among the five most common street names, is **Station Road**. It is difficult to pin down exactly how many Station Roads there are in Britain; estimates vary from around 1,600 to over 3,800. There are 2,563 railways stations in Britain today and if you assume that every one of them has a Station Road associated with it, then you arrive at a figure somewhere between those two extremes. In Victorian times there were many more stations than exist today, and many Station Roads survive in communities that no longer have a station. One example is Station Road in the village of Scrooby, Nottinghamshire, whose station closed in 1931. It is now a quiet country lane leading to nowhere - but it is not without history: it runs past the old manor house where William Brewster, spiritual leader of the Mayflower Pilgrim Fathers and founder of Plymouth Colony in America, was born in 1567.

AVENUE

A 'roadway with trees or other objects at regular intervals, broad street'. Avenues are usually associated in people's minds with trees and upmarket houses. The word 'avenue' comes from the French *avenir*, derived in turn from the Latin *advenire*, meaning 'to come' or 'to approach', and the first avenues were usually tree-lined and led up to a country house or architectural feature on a large estate.

Avenue is a very common type of street name, both as a specific and a suffix, and there are over six hundred roads in Britain called **The Avenue**. Since avenues are associated with grand country estates, many suburban residential streets are called 'avenues' to make them seem more rural and imposing than they really are. Even major urban roads may be called an avenue, such as the **Western Avenue** in London, which is actually part of the grime-filled, traffic-choked A40.

As well as The Avenue, the most common name for such a street is **Park Avenue**, illustrating how avenues are associated with more formal settings, again evoking a grand country estate. A street called The Avenue, for instance, promotes the idea that this must be the most desirable street in the area.

BOULEVARD

A 'broad street with rows of trees along it', 'boulevard' is a French term derived from the German *Bollwerk* (bulwark). Indeed, a boulevard originally followed the line of a defensive fortification or bulwark, and this is still sometimes the case. In Nottingham, for instance, **Castle Boulevard** runs along the line of the defensive walls of the old castle, and joins with **Gregory Boulevard**, **Radford Boulevard** and **Lenton Boulevard** to make a tree-lined ring road around the medieval walls of the city. The Victorian councillors who had the ring road built favoured boulevards as they wanted their bypass to be a thing of grandeur and beauty rather than just another traffic-filled road. In a similar spirit, the city's famous son Jesse Boot (see page 170) funded **University Boulevard** in the 1930s as a grand road to Beeston. Nottingham is unusual for a British city in having so many boulevards, a type of street more commonly associated with the wide, tree-bedecked avenues of Paris with their wide pavements and open-air cafés. Surprisingly, these Parisian boulevards were actually inspired by a Great British street, **Lord Street** in Southport on Merseyside, which was named after the joint lords of the manor who built it, the Bold-Houghton and Fleetwood-Hesketh families. Prince Louis-Napoléon Bonaparte, a nephew of Napoleon, lived on Lord Street for a while in the 1840s and was clearly impressed with the spaciousness of the street and the plentiful trees, gardens, fountains and memorials that lined it. When he returned to France to become Emperor Napoleon III in 1851, he had the old narrow streets of the centre of Paris demolished and replaced with the broad boulevards, reminiscent of Lord Street in Southport, that we know today.

The only other town in Britain to have more than one or two boulevards is the 'new town' of Milton Keynes in Buckinghamshire, although it is possible to drive along the odd British boulevard elsewhere. **Highland Boulevard** in Leigh-on-Sea in Essex qualifies as it has a grass central reservation. **Mosspark Boulevard** in Glasgow is indeed tree-lined. Aberdeen's **Beach Boulevard** is wide, with a central reservation, and leads down to the beach. **Boulevard** in Weston-super-Mare in Somerset is wide, with the odd tree, and also leads down to the sea, which gives it a certain glamour mildly reminiscent of Boulevard de la Croisette in Cannes in the south of France, if one is being generous - without the palm trees, of course. **Sunset Boulevard** in Warrington is pushing it a bit, although it does head west towards the sunset and has lots of bends in it, like the rather more glamorous Sunset Boulevard in Los Angeles. **Boulevard De Nantes** in Cardiff, a wide, tree-lined street that runs past the Civic Centre, is named after the French city with which Cardiff is twinned. **Boulevard De Saint Brieuc** in Aberystwyth is also named for its twin town, as is **Bourges Boulevard** in Peterborough.

SMALL ROADS

LANE

A 'narrow road, usually between hedges'. Lanes used to be found mostly in the countryside and, as we saw on page 12, the word comes from the Old English or Anglo-Saxon *lane* or *lanu*, a general term used for the unnamed paths, tracks and byways that criss-crossed England, many of which are now known as 'green lanes'. Indeed, most people's idea of a lane is a rural road, as in a 'country lane', but as towns and cities have spread into the countryside, many lanes have become built up while retaining their Lane suffix. Since urbanisation the term 'lane' is now recognised also as 'a narrow road or street between houses or walls, a bye-way'. Many such urban lanes have become fashionable as shopping and eating areas, such as **The Lanes** in Brighton and Glasgow's **West End Lanes**.

The most common name for a lane is **Church Lane**, which is hardly surprising since Britain has been a Christian country for some 1,500 years and virtually every community is centred around a church, which is usually the oldest and most important building in that community. There are some 40,000 churches in Britain of all denominations, more than any other type of public building. **Church Street** and **Church Road** are also among the top ten street names, but Church Lane is more common because, until the nineteenth century, there were more country churches than urban ones and Lane is a more common suffix in the country. Dozens of other suffixes also appear with the name Church, often describing a no-through way, such as **Church End**, **Church Walk**, **Church Close** and **Church Acre**, reflecting how the church usually stands at the centre of the community, as the first building to have been erected, with all roads leading to it or radiating from it.

Penny Lane, Liverpool. Perhaps the most famous lane in the world thanks to the Beatles, Penny Lane can be found in the Liverpool suburb of Mossley Hill. It is a good example of a country lane that became urbanised when it was lined with rows of terraced houses in the 1890s.

In the 1950s there was a major bus terminus at one end of the lane where, as youngsters, John Lennon and Paul McCartney would change buses when they visited each other's houses, and in 1967 the Beatles released the eponymous song in which John and Paul recalled the people and businesses they had observed while hanging around the bus shelter. Because it was released as a double A-side single with 'Strawberry Fields Forever', 'Penny Lane' only reached No. 2 in the British charts since the number of sales was effectively halved by being split between the two songs, but it did reach No. 1 in America and has remained one of the Beatles most popular songs internationally, bringing fans from all over the world to see the lane that inspired the song. The 'Penny Lane' street signs were so frequently stolen by fans that the council began painting the name on walls and the sides of buildings instead, but this gave rise to so many complaints that officials relented and put up signs that were more difficult to remove.

In 2020 there was something of a ruckus when it was suggested that Penny Lane might have been named after a prominent eighteenth-century slave trader called James Penny. The signs were vandalised and there was a movement to have the name changed, much to the distress of Beatles fans. Liverpool's International Slavery Museum, however, has found no evidence linking Penny Lane to James Penny, who was not a Liverpudlian, and local people have always believed that the lane was named for a penny toll that was put across the road when it formed an important route into Liverpool.

ALLEY

See the next chapter. Alleys are so varied and interesting that I feel they deserve their own chapter.

ARCADE

Originally a covered alleyway, an arcade is now more commonly used to describe a covered shopping street. From the Latin *arcus*, meaning 'bow', which led to the Italian *arcata*, meaning 'arch'.

Burlington Arcade, off Piccadilly in London, is Britain's longest arcade and one of the country's earliest, opening in 1819. It began life as an alleyway running alongside Burlington House, but the Earl of Burlington objected to people throwing rubbish over the wall into his garden, so he arranged for the alleyway to be covered over. Shops were added so that his wife could shop in safety away from the dirty streets and out of the rain. The earl hired former members of his regiment, the 10th Royal Hussars, to patrol the arcade. Known as 'beadles', they could be said to have been Britain's first police force, and they still watch over the arcade today.

PARADE

A street lined with shops, 'parade' derives from the Latin *parare*, meaning 'to prepare' or 'to show', hence a display or 'show' of shops.

COMMON

A road that runs alongside an area of common land, usually named after the common itself. The word comes from the Latin *communis*, meaning 'belonging to all'. Also **Green**, a local road lined with gardens or a public green space, like a village green. Also **Park**, a local road running adjacent to a park or gardens. From the medieval Latin *parricus* via Old French *parc*, meaning a pen or paddock - originally a term used by the Norman kings for an enclosed area of land held by royal grant for keeping animals. Essentially an enclosed common.

DRIVE
From the Old English *drifan*, meaning 'to urge forward', as a drover would urge forward or drive his cattle between farm and field or the market. A drive is usually an upmarket residential road with a view and is also used to describe a private road leading to a house. Also **View**, a road that offers a scenic view, such as **River View**, **Hill View** or **Park View**. It can often be appear with Drive as a suffix, such as **Mountain View Drive**.

GARDEN OR GARDENS
Local road lined by houses with gardens or built on the former gardens of a larger property. Also **Garth**, from the Old Norse *garthr*, meaning 'yard' or 'enclosure', such as **Palmers Garth**, Durham, on the site of an enclosure where pilgrims would camp. Pilgrims were sometimes known as 'palmers' because they would bring back palm leaves as proof of a pilgrimage to the Holy Land. Also **Grove**, from the Old English *graf*, meaning 'small wood'; **Lea**, from the Old English *lea*, referring to a tract of open grassland; **Orchard**, a local road running through a former orchard or gardens; and **Wood** or **Woods**, a street adjacent to a wood or constructed on former woodland.

ROW
From the Anglo-Saxon *raw*, referring to individuals or things arranged in a line, hence a road that follows a line or row of houses. Also **Cottages**, leading to a group or row of cottages.

* **Crynfryn Row**, Aberystwyth. Named after a house, Y Crynfryn, the home of the man who built the street, Sir Thomas Bonsall (1730-1808).

TERRACE

A street that follows a line or row of terraced houses. 'Terrace' comes from the French *terrasse*, referring to a levelled area or flattened earth (derived in turn from the Latin *terra*, meaning 'earth'). Terraced houses were originally built on a terrace, but a terrace now tends to describe a row of joined-up houses built in a uniform block and of uniform architectural style.

CUL DE SAC

The term comes from the French expression meaning 'bottom, or closed end, of a sack', hence a cul de sac is a street with one end closed and the other end open, just like a sack. Also **No-Through Road**, **Dead End** and **Blind Alley**.

CLOSE

From the Latin *clausum*, meaning 'enclosure', a close is an enclosed residential street and Close is now the most popular form of suffix for this type of street. Similar suffixes for enclosed residential streets are **Court**, **Courtyard**, **Corner**, **Place**, **Croft** and **End**.

* **Vicars' Close**, Wells, Somerset. Laid out in the mid-fourteenth century to provide accommodation for the chantry priests of Wells Cathedral, this extraordinarily beautiful short street is the oldest planned residential street to survive intact in the whole of Europe.

ROADS NAMED FOR THEIR SHAPE

CIRCUS

From the Latin *circulus*, meaning 'ring' or 'circle', a circus is usually a junction or roundabout where roads converge.

* **The Circus**, Bath, Somerset. The world's most beautiful circus and the ultimate manifestation of the Georgian love of architectural rectangles, squares and circles, The Circus was built between 1756 and 1768 by John Wood the Younger to the design of his father, John Wood the Elder. It is formed of three curved terraces of equal length with an embowered circular lawn at the centre. The three entrance roads each face the centre of a terrace, thus ensuring that each approach has a classical vista. Not just a glorious piece of architecture, The Circus has a deep symbolic significance. It is the same diameter as Stonehenge, thirty miles away, while, from above, The Circus, in conjunction with **Gay Street** and **Queen Square** to the south, form the shape of a key, an important Masonic symbol.

* **Circus Lane**, Stockbridge, Edinburgh. This street behind the **Royal Circus** in Edinburgh's Georgian New Town is really a mews (see page 28), for the houses in Circus Lane were built as accommodation with stables for the Royal Circus. It is frequently voted Scotland's prettiest street.

* **Piccadilly Circus**, London. Laid out in 1819 at the junction of the newly built Regent Street on Piccadilly, this was originally just a crossroads but when Regent Street was designed on a grand scale, it was decided to set back the four corners and line the junction with curved buildings to create a circular space to be

known as Regent Circus South, Regent Circus North being what is now **Oxford Circus**. The Piccadilly circle was destroyed when the buildings in the north-east section were pulled down to accommodate **Shaftesbury Avenue**, and the whole area has been completely remodelled over the years so that it is now difficult to discern a circle at all. In 1893 a memorial fountain crowned with the world's first aluminium public statue was unveiled at the centre of the circus. Representing the Angel of Christian Charity, it was a tribute to the philanthropist and social reformer Lord Shaftesbury (1801-85). The statue is actually of the Greek god of requited love, Anteros, but is generally referred to as Eros, his somewhat better-known brother. Eros originally faced north up Shaftesbury Avenue, named for Lord Shaftesbury, but after the statue was removed for safety during the Second World War, it was put back facing the wrong way, south-west. Red-faced officials blustered that they had meant to do that all along as Eros was now facing towards Lord Shaftesbury's country home in Dorset.

CRESCENT

A street lined with houses that forms the shape of an arc. The word 'crescent' comes from the Latin *crescere*, meaning 'to grow', and was used to describe the shape of the new or 'growing' moon, *luna crescens*. Crescents, like squares (see opposite), are very much a feature of Georgian and Regency architecture. The most common name for a crescent is . . . **The Crescent**.

* **Royal Crescent**, Bath, Somerset. Five hundred feet in length and forming a perfect half-circle, the Royal Crescent was the first crescent of terraced houses ever to be constructed. Built between 1767 and 1774 by John Wood the Younger, it was originally named simply The Crescent (like The Circus above) but became the Royal Crescent after Prince Frederick, Duke of York and Albany, second

son of George III, stayed in No. 1 at the end of the eighteenth century and later bought No. 16. As Stonehenge honours the rising and setting sun, so The Circus represents the sun while the Royal Crescent represents the crescent moon.

* **Royal York Crescent**, Clifton, Bristol. At 1,280 feet in length, this is the world's longest unbroken crescent. The longest crescent complex is **Lansdown Crescent** in Cheltenham, Gloucestershire, which is 1,663 feet in length.

SQUARE

An open area in the shape of a square, often the central feature of a town and a meeting place for events and gatherings.

* **Leicester Square**, London. Leicester Square was formerly Leicester Fields, a patch of open land to the south of Leicester House, which was built in 1635 for Robert Sidney, 2nd Earl of Leicester, who in 1670 had the fields transformed into a square, 'for the decency of the place before Leicester House'. Over the years, Leicester House had a number of distinguished residents, including George II's son Frederick, Prince of Wales, who moved in after he was chucked out of St James's Palace by his father. Successive Hanoverian heirs to the throne, all of whom fell out with their fathers, set up an alternative court at Leicester House, and their followers became known as the Leicester House faction. Eventually the Prince Regent, the future George IV, sold the house to help pay off his debts, and it was demolished in 1791, the whole area subsequently redeveloped as a commercial district. In 1874 the square was purchased by the flamboyant and controversial entrepreneur Baron Grant, who donated it to the people of London. During the Victorian era, theatres were put up which were then converted to cinemas in the twentieth century, and today the square remains at the heart of London's West End entertainment quarter.

ROADS NAMED FOR THEIR PHYSICAL LOCATION

BANK

Either a street that runs along a river bank or a street lined by a row of houses, the term derived in each case from the Old Norse *bakki*, meaning a river bank or a hill.

DALE

Meaning 'valley', particularly in northern England, from Old English (*dael*) or Old Norse (*dalr*). Also **Dell**. Also **Hollow**, from the Old English *hohl*, meaning an unfilled space or hole. The suffix Hollow is usually applied to a road whose surface is below the banks on either side. Also **Vale**, another word for 'valley', particularly in southern England.

FIELD OR FIELDS

Local road built over former fields. Also **Meadow**, a piece of grassland, especially near a river, from the Old English *mædwe*. Local road built where there were meadows. Also **Mead**, another word for 'meadow'.

HILL

Street on a hill. Also **Ridge**, **Rise** and **Mount**.

ROADS NAMED FOR THEIR FUNCTION

APPROACH

From the Latin *appropiare*, meaning 'to draw near', Approach, like Avenue, is a street that leads to a landmark or building, as in **Station Approach** or **Church Approach**.

ESPLANADE

A level space separating a fortress or citadel from the town to provide an unobstructed line of fire for the defences, from the Latin *planare*, 'to make level'. In modern parlance, an esplanade is a level piece of ground, usually by the sea, for people to promenade along. The seaside towns of Redcar, Exmouth and Aberdeen each have an esplanade. In fact there are over forty Esplanades in Britain, all of them by the sea. Esplanades became popular in Britain in the nineteenth century when seaside towns no longer required fortifications and became places of leisure and entertainment. One of the first was **Weymouth Esplanade**, which curves around the shore of Weymouth Bay and is backed by smart Georgian and Regency terraces (see page 22). It was from the beach off Weymouth Esplanade that George III made sea bathing fashionable in 1789 by becoming the first monarch to use a bathing machine: as he dipped a royal toe into the water, a band hidden in an adjacent machine struck up 'God Save the King'! Aberdeen's **North Esplanade East** runs along the banks of the River Dee.

PROMENADE

A 'place to walk' especially by the seaside, from the French *promener*, 'to walk'. A promenade is more or less synonymous with an esplanade although among Britain's thirty or so promenades there are a number of inland ones. **The Promenade** in Cheltenham in Gloucestershire was built in 1818 as somewhere for the wealthy visitors who came to sample Cheltenham's spa waters to 'promenade' and be seen.

WALK

Like a promenade, this describes a track or way laid out to be suitable for walking, although not necessarily just for pedestrians. Indeed, it can be used by any form of traffic unless specifically prohibited (see overleaf).

* **Lambeth Walk**, London. Famous as a cockney dance and song made popular by Lupino Lane in the 1937 musical *Me and My Girl*, Lambeth Walk was noted in the nineteenth century for its extensive market which at one time boasted 164 costermongers. Charlie Chaplin (1889-1977), known for his iconic screen character 'The Tramp', was born and grew up in abject poverty in Lambeth, and is remembered by a series of mosaics on the wall of the Chandler Community Hall at 15 Lambeth Walk. The nearby Lambeth Workhouse where Chaplin lived as a child when his mother was destitute is now home to the Cinema Museum.

* **Leith Walk**, Edinburgh. Edinburgh's longest street stretches between the city centre and the harbour at Leith. It runs along the line of a medieval rampart and was originally prohibited to horses and wheeled traffic.

GATE

See the 'Gates' chapter on page 44.

MEWS

Stables with accommodation above for the stable hands and coachmen, located at the back of large townhouses. Mews are invariably quiet, pretty and cobbled and the converted stables known as mews houses have now become hugely desirable properties. The word comes from the French *muer*, meaning 'to moult or shed feathers', from the Latin *mutare*, meaning 'to change'. The first Mews was the King's Mews at Charing Cross in London where the royal hawks were confined while they were moulting. The mews burned down in 1534 and the royal stables were built on the site but the name King's Mews was kept and from then on the term 'mews' was applied to stables. Most Mews are found in London. London's first petrol pump was installed in **Queen's Gate Mews** in Kensington in 1913, the name of which might be why the 'Queen of Pop', Madonna, once had a house in the street. Agatha Christie lived in **Cresswell Mews** in Chelsea and used the street as the setting for her 1937 novel *Murder in the Mews*. A property in Marylebone's **Bryanston Mews**, which takes its name from the Dorset home of the landlords, the Portman family (see page 152), was once owned by the notorious slum landlord Peter Rachman, and it was here that he conducted his affairs with Christine Keeler and Mandy Rice Davies in the days before the Profumo scandal in the early 1960s. The two girls later lived nearby in the notorious **Wimpole Mews** in the home of Stephen Ward, the doctor who introduced them to high society. It was there that Keeler slept with Secretary of State for War John Profumo and where Stephen Ward later committed suicide.

QUAY

A 'solid stationary artificial landing place lying alongside, or projecting into, water, for unloading ships'. From the Middle English *key* and Old French *kay*, later influenced by the modern French spelling, *quai*.

* **South Quay**, Great Yarmouth, Norfolk. Daniel Defoe described Great Yarmouth's South Quay as 'the finest quay in England, if not in Europe'. It runs along the River Yare, sheltered from the North Sea by a narrow spit of land on which stands a fine array of Elizabethan and Georgian merchant's houses. One of these is home to the only museum anywhere solely dedicated to Admiral Lord Nelson. After he landed in Great Yarmouth fresh from his victory at the Battle of the Nile in 1798 (see page 122), he was offered the freedom of the town and as he put his left hand on the proffered Bible, the clerk said, 'Your right hand, please, my Lord.' 'That,' replied Nelson, 'is in Tenerife.'

* Manchester has **Salford Quays**, home to the BBC studios, running alongside the Manchester Ship Canal. Portsmouth in Hampshire has

Gunwharf Quays on the harbour waterfront, where naval cannon, guns, ammunition and other armaments were stored and serviced ready for use at sea. Cardiff has **Britannia Quay** on Cardiff Bay and Aberdeen has **Albert Quay**, **Regent Quay** and **Commercial Quay**, all running along the dockside.

VIADUCT

From the Latin *via*, meaning 'way', and *ducere*, meaning 'to lead', this is an elevated road or railway supported by a bridge that crosses an obstacle, such as a valley or another road.

* **Holborn Viaduct**, London. A street that includes, and is named after, the viaduct built in the 1860s to bridge the dangerously steep valley of the River Fleet. The actual Holborn Viaduct is sometimes described as the world's first flyover. The lights set in the six cast-iron lamp standards on the viaduct were originally powered by electricity from the world's first public coal-fired electricity-generating station, which was opened nearby in 1882 by Thomas Edison. Holborn takes its name from the Hole Bourne ('stream in the hollow'), a tributary of the River Fleet.

2

ALLEYS

ALLEY OR ALLEYWAY

A 'narrow street or passage', 'alley' comes from the French *aller*, meaning 'to go'. Alleys or alleyways are very often among the oldest and most historic streets in a town or city, and frequently the most interesting. Their colourful names can reveal a lot about the history, culture and everyday life of a town.

* **Exchange Alley** or **Change Alley** in the City of London, one of the many narrow passages that run between the Royal Exchange on Cornhill and the banks of Lombard Street. These passages, and this alleyway in particular, were the original information superhighways. In the seventeenth and eighteenth centuries, bankers, merchants and traders would meet in the new coffee houses along them to exchange financial news and ideas. Jonathan's on Exchange Alley, for instance, was the original stock exchange.

* The dark and dingy **Passing Alley** in London's Clerkenwell was, in the bawdy 'tell it like it is' days of the eighteenth century, known as Pissing Alley, no doubt since it was used as a caught-short cut for gentlemen falling out of the local taverns to relieve themselves. As more delicate sensibilities kicked in, the name was subtly altered.

* **Pope's Head Alley**, York's narrowest alleyway, only two and a half feet wide in places, is named after a pub that stood nearby, as is Pope's Head Alley in London. The London Pope's Head apparently changed its name to Bishop's Head for a while after the Reformation.

PASS, PATH AND PASSAGE

There are many different ways of describing what is essentially an alley, such as Pass, Path or Passage, examples of the latter being **Jeffries Passage** in Guildford, Surrey, which was named after a

Victorian chemist, Henry Jeffries, who had his shop in the alleyway. Likewise **Camden Passage** in Islington, an alleyway that runs along the backs of the shops and houses in Upper Street, formerly part of Islington High Street. Famous for its antique shops, it is named after local landowner Sir Charles Pratt, the 1st Earl Camden (1714-94), whose earldom was styled after his estate in Chislehurst, Camden Place, which was in turn named after a previous owner, the historian William Camden (1551-1623).

STEPS

Some alleyways are accessed by steps and thus attract the suffix Steps. One example is **Christmas Steps** in Bristol, where a set of steps leads down to a steep, narrow cobbled street lined with quirky shops. Laid out in 1669, this is one of the few ancient streets to survive in the centre of Bristol and, being the street where knife makers and cutlers plied their trade, was known as Knyfesmyth Street, which evolved into Christmas Street and eventually, for the stepped part of the street, Christmas Steps.

TWITTEN, TWITCHELL AND FOLLEY

In Sussex and southern England, an alley may sometimes be called a 'twitten', meaning 'a narrow path between two walls or hedges'. It seems to come from the Anglo-Saxon *twicen*, describing a place where two roads meet, and *twitchel*, a forked road, leading to the idea of a narrow alleyway that runs between two roads. **Twitcher's Alley** in Bicester in Oxfordshire combines the two.

In Brighton, twittens tend to be lined with cottages and gardens and, apparently, one can walk from one side of Old Brighton to the other just using the twittens. They are notoriously narrow and on one occasion, as an anonymous nineteenth-century contributor to the *Derbyshire Advertiser and Journal* tells us, the portly Prince

Regent, who when staying at the Brighton Pavilion liked to walk along the narrow twittens early in the morning before breakfast, was negotiating one of the narrower alleyways when he came face to face with a lady 'no less remarkable for her *embonpoint* than the Prince himself'. They could not pass or turn around and so the prince, ever the gentleman, doffed his hat and retreated slowly back down the twitten to the road, courteously stood aside as the lady emerged, and then re-entered the alley and resumed his morning constitutional.

In Lewes in Sussex, twittens tend to be narrow passageways that run between high walls, the best example being **Church Twitten**, which runs from the High Street down to the parish church. The tiny Sussex town of Cuckfield also has a Church Twitten and the rather wonderfully named **Mytten Twitten**, so called after Mytten House, built in the 1830s as the family home of Thomas Ashley Maberley, the vicar of Cuckfield between 1841 and 1877.

In Essex and the eastern counties of England, a 'twitten' becomes a 'twitchell'. In Colchester, Essex, there are a number of alleyways called 'folley', as in **Artillery Barracks Folley** and **North Camp Folley**, although no one seems to know where the word 'folley' comes from or why they seem to be particularly associated with military camps. I could hazard a guess that it might come from the Old French *feuillie*, meaning 'leafy bower or shelter', hence a leafy way through a camp site.

DRANGWAY

In the West Country and parts of South Wales, an alleyway can be known as 'drangway', *drang* being a Devon dialect word for 'crowd' or 'throng', which seems to come from the German *dringen*, meaning 'to press', hence a way that is so narrow as to cause a throng or press of people.

OPE

The West Country port towns of Plymouth and Truro have alleyways running from the old city centre to the waterfront called 'opes', short for 'opening' but pronounced 'op'. Most of the opes in Plymouth are named after the road off which they open, such as **Adelaide Street Ope**, named after Queen Adelaide, wife of the 'Sailor King', William IV, or the self-explanatory **Admiralty Street Ope North** and **Admiralty Street Ope South**. Slightly more interesting are **Basket Ope**, an alley where baskets were made, and **Blackfriars Ope**, named after the Black Friars monastery where many of the Pilgrim Fathers stayed in 1620 while waiting for the *Mayflower* to be prepared. The site is now occupied by Britain's oldest working gin distillery, the Plymouth Gin Distillery. In Truro the opes are named after local people, examples being **Roberts Ope**, **Pearsons Ope** and **Swifty's Ope**, named after a local artist. **Carne's Ope**, lost in the 1960s but now rediscovered, was named after the nearby Carnes brewery. Just to confuse, Mevagissey in Cornwall boasts a **Shilly Alley Op** with the 'Op' spelled as it is pronounced (try saying the name after a pint of Cornish ale). The name is probably a mischievous play on words, from the expression 'shilly shally' meaning to vacillate or act indecisively (from the eighteenth-century expression 'Shill I? Shall I?'). Since the entrance to the ope is fairly well hidden, people do sometimes hesitate before starting down the narrow street and so the name is eminently fitting.

SHUT OR SHUTT

In Shropshire, an alleyway between two main streets that passes between or underneath buildings is called a 'shut'. Shrewsbury, the county town, still has a network of ancient shuts running between the busy streets of the town centre. They serve as useful short cuts, suggesting that 'shut' may be a contraction of 'short cut'. Some examples of Shrewsbury shuts are:

* **Bowdler's Passage**, named after the prominent local family of Bowdler, one of whom, Thomas Bowdler, was mayor of Shrewsbury in 1705. A later member of the same family was the physician Thomas Bowdler (1754-1825), whose famous expurgated version of Shakespeare led to the expression 'bowdlerise'.

* **Carnarvon Lane**, named after a local merchant from the fifteenth century called Ludovick Carnarvon.

* **Coffee House Passage**, named after an eighteenth-century coffee house where coffee was stored and sold that stood at the top of the street.

* **Compasses Passage**, named after the Compasses Inn that stood here, a timber-framed building with illustrations of carpenter's tools, including compasses, carved into the timbers.

* **Golden Cross Passage**, named after the Golden Cross Hotel, the oldest pub in Shrewsbury.

* **Phoenix Place**, named after a popular Victorian baker called Mr Phoenix who had his shop here.

Much Wenlock, also in Shropshire, has **The Mutton Shut**, which, presumably, was a short cut to the meat market.

In South Wales, 'shutts' are spelled with a double 't'. The meaning seems to be a boundary or enclosure, as in somewhere 'shut in', suggesting that a shut runs along the boundary of an enclosed plot of land, especially in the town.

JITTY AND GULLEY

In the Midland counties of Leicestershire and Derbyshire, an alley may be known as a 'jitty', while in Worcestershire, the Black Country and the counties of the Welsh Marches the term 'gulley' is used, from the Middle English *golet*, referring to a water channel or stream, as in 'gully'. A good example is **Gullet Passage** in Shrewsbury, a narrow street or 'shut' that follows the course of a stream that used to run from the town centre down to the River Severn.

GINNEL, GENNEL AND SNICKET

In Yorkshire and Lancashire an alley can be known as a 'ginnel' - often used by characters in the long-running Manchester-based soap opera *Coronation Street* (see page 143) - 'gennel' or, in York, 'snicket'. A snicket is an alleyway between walls or fences, while a ginnel is an alleyway between buildings. In 1983, in his book *A Walk Around the Snickelways of York*, local author Mark W. Jones combined 'snicket' with 'ginnel' and 'alleyway' to produce **snickelway**, a term that has found favour with York folk and even with York officials. York is full of such snickelways, many with intriguing names.

* **Bedern Passage** leads to the fourteenth-century Bedern Chapel, all that remains of the College of the Vicars Choral of York Minster.

* **Coffee Yard**, where coffee was stored and traded, is York's longest snickelway.

* **Grape Lane**, a sanitised name for what was originally Grope Lane (see page 198), where indelicate activities took place. Durham and a number of other towns have similar Grape Lanes.

* **Lady Peckett's Yard** is named for Alice Peckett, wife of an early eighteenth-century Lord Mayor of York.

* **Little Peculiar Lane**, York's shortest snickelway, led to Minster Yard, an ecclesiastical 'peculiar'. A peculiar is a parish or church body outside the jurisdiction of the bishop and subject to a jurisdiction 'peculiar' to itself. Westminster Abbey, for instance, is a royal peculiar, which means that it does not come under the jurisdiction of the Bishop of London but rather of the abbey's Dean and Chapter on behalf of the monarch. 'Peculiar' comes from the Latin *peculium*, meaning 'private property', particularly that gifted by an authority to a junior person or body. In church terms, the pope would often grant peculiars in order to curtail the power of a bishop.

* **Mad Alice Lane** is reputedly named after a woman called Alice who was hanged in 1823 for murdering her husband, despite pleading insanity, although no record can be found of her execution so this story may have been embroidered slightly - Alice may just have been an eccentric!

* **Nether Hornpot Lane** refers to the horn makers who had their workshops there.

GHAUT

In Whitby in North Yorkshire, a narrow alleyway that leads from the street down to the waterfront is known locally as a 'ghaut', from the Middle English *gote*, meaning a drain or channel (similar to 'gutter'). A famous example was **Tin Ghaut**, which didn't have anything to do with tin but was the 'ghaut next t'inn', Yorkshire for 'next to the inn'. Some ghauts still exist but tend to have been subsumed into lanes and given more standard names today.

CHARE

In the north-east of England, particularly Newcastle upon Tyne, an alleyway was known as a 'chare', from the Anglo-Saxon word *cer* or *cerre*, meaning a turning (off a street). Most chares have disappeared, but Newcastle still has a few, such as **Cox Chare**, **Pudding Chare** and **Trinity Chare**, while others include Bishop Auckland's **Durham Chare** and **Gib Chare**. Durham has **Castle Chare** and Morpeth, **Copper Chare**.

JIGGER AND ENTRY

Liverpudlians might call an alleyway a 'jigger' - based on the dialect word *jig*, describing something small or narrow - or an 'entry'.
In working-class areas, people would often enter their houses through the back door rather than the front, thus the alleyways at the back of houses were the 'entries' rather than the streets at the front.

In the heart of old Belfast, which has strong historic ties to Liverpool, there is a group of alleyways running off the High Street that are known as the **Belfast Entries**, since they were the entryways to various commercial ventures or residences. They are among the oldest streets in the city.

* **Castle Arcade** led to the castle.

* **Crown Entry** is named for the Crown Tavern, which is reputed to be where Wolfe Tone formed the Society of United Irishmen in 1791.

* **Joy's Entry** is named in honour of Francis Joy (1697-1790), founder in 1737 of the *News Letter*, the oldest newspaper in the world still in circulation.

* **Pottinger's Entry** is named after a prominent local family, the Pottingers. Sir Henry Pottinger (1789-1856) became the first Governor of Hong Kong in 1843.

* **Sugar House Entry** was the way to the sugarhouse where sugar was processed and traded.

* **Winecellar Entry** leads to Belfast's oldest pub, White's Tavern, founded in 1630.

SCOTTISH ALLEYWAYS

In Scotland there are a number of terms for different types of alleyway.

CLOSE

'Close' is the generic term for an alleyway, although it also describes a private or 'closed' alleyway. There are a number of closes off the Royal Mile in Edinburgh.

* **Advocates Close** is named after Sir James Stewart, Lord Advocate of Scotland in the early eighteenth century, who had a house there.

* **Big Jack's Close** off Canongate is named after eighteenth-century landowner and magistrate John Jack.

* **Brodie's Close** is named for the home of Deacon Brodie, an eighteenth-century cabinet maker and councillor who moonlighted as a thief to fund his gambling.

* **Gibb's Close** is named after Robert Gibb, who had stables there. In 1928, body snatchers William Burke and William Hare murdered Mary Paterson so that they could sell her corpse to the anatomist Dr Robert Knox for dissection.

* **Lady Stair's Close** off Lawnmarket, is named after Lady Stair's

House, owned by Elizabeth Dundas (1650-1731), widow of the 1st Earl of Stair.

* **Mary King's Close**, off the High Street and reputedly haunted, is named after a seventeenth-century merchant who lived in the close.

* **Old Distillery Close**, off Castlehill is, fittingly, home to the Scotch Whisky Experience.

* **Old Playhouse Close** led to the Playhouse Theatre.

* **World's End Close** was the last close before the old town wall.

PEND

A 'pend' is an alleyway that passes through or under a building. The word comes from the Latin *pendere*, meaning to hang (hence words such as 'pendulous' and 'pendulum'), seeing as an arch or a vault, or in this case a building, might hang over a passageway. **St John's Pend**, off Canongate on the Royal Mile in Edinburgh, recalls that this is where the Knights of St John had their houses.

VENNEL

A 'vennel' is an alleyway between buildings and comes from the Old French word for an alley, *venelle*, from the Latin *venella*, meaning 'funnel'. There is an alley called simply **Vennel**, leading from Heriot Row to the Grassmarket in Edinburgh.

WYND

My favourite term for an alley, however, is 'wynd', since it opens up so many possibilities. Prevalent in Scotland and the north of England, 'wynd' comes from the Old Norse word *venda*, meaning 'to wander' or 'to wend', and refers to a narrow lane that wends its way between houses of differing heights. **Correction Wynd** in Aberdeen stands on the site of a seventeenth-century house of correction, where vagrants were sent to work. **Old Tolbooth Wynd** off Canongate on Edinburgh's Royal Mile refers to the tolbooth that served variously as council offices, parliament, courthouse and prison. **Bull Wynd** in Darlington is named after the Bulmer family who ran a nearby inn. **Post House Wynd** in Darlington stands on the site of the stables of the long-gone Post House Inn.

In Dundee, the 'wynds' are named after professions or members of a profession (see also page 86).

* **Bucklemaker Wynd**, as it used to be called, was changed in the nineteenth century to **Victoria Street** in honour of Queen Victoria.

* **Couttie's Wynd**, a narrow street that runs between the back of the houses of Dundee's main streets, Union Street and Whitehall Street, is named after a sixteenth-century butcher, William Couttie.

* **Miller's Wynd** winds through the old mill district of Dundee and presumably is named after the millers in general, or possibly a family called Miller after their profession.

* **Small's Wynd**, also in the mill district, could be named after a family of millers called Small or Smalls. There is also a **Small's Lane** adjacent.

Along with the suffixes Entry, Bottom and Passage, Wynd has produced some amusing street names for those of a certain turn of mind. I refer, of course, to Aberdeen's peerless **Back Wynd**, Edinburgh's **Horse Wynd** and St Andrews' rather splendid **Butts Wynd**. Mind you, the childish humour is tempered somewhat when one realises that 'wynd' is pronounced 'wined' not 'wind'. Ah well.

3

GATES

'Gate' comes from the Old Norse *gata*, meaning 'street' (in Scotland and the north), or the Old English *geat*, meaning 'gate', as in a gateway in a wall (in the south).

'Gates' are usually the oldest streets in a town or city. For example, **Great Darkgate Street**, in Aberystwyth, is the original east-west artery through the town and is named after the Great Gate in the town hall. **Eastgate** is Chester's oldest street and leads to the East Gate, the original main gateway to the Roman fort of Deva. Atop the present eighteenth-century gate is the Eastgate Clock, put up in 1899 to celebrate the diamond jubilee of Queen Victoria.

SCOTLAND

ABERDEEN

Aberdeen had six medieval gateways or 'ports' in the walls protecting the old castle. The castle was destroyed by Robert the Bruce in the fourteenth century but is remembered by **Castle Street**, **Castle Terrace** and the central Castlegate area. By the middle of the eighteenth century, all of the gates had been demolished because they obstructed traffic - but their memory lives on in names of the streets that passed through them. The Hardgate, part of which survives today as **Hardgate**, was the main road out of Aberdeen to the south across the Brig O'Dee, and one of the few stone or 'hard' streets in the medieval city. **Upperkirkgate** runs above the Mother Kirk of St Nicholas, while **Netherkirkgate**, the oldest named street in Aberdeen, runs below the church ('nether' meaning 'below' - see also 'Dundee' on page 46). **Gallowgate**, near to the site of the old market gallows, which were used both for weighing market produce and hanging miscreants, guarded the castle from the north. The former Trinity Gate at the waterfront is recalled by **Trinity Quay**, and the original Justice Gate, where the justices had their lodgings, by **Justice Street**. Futty Port and its corresponding street, Futty Wynd, are, alas, no more. *Futty* (or *fitty*) is an Old Scottish word for 'expeditious' and the Futty Port was most likely used to 'expedite' the entry and exit of soldiers from the castle.

DUNDEE

* **Marketgait** follows the 'way to the market', while cattle were led to market along **Cowgate**. The ruined Cowgate or East Port, set within a remnant of the sixteenth-century city walls on Cowgate, is Dundee's only surviving old gateway.

* **Murraygate** is named in honour of Robert the Bruce's nephew Thomas Randolph, 1st Earl of Moray, who visited Dundee in 1314 and entered the town along the way that now bears his name.

* **Nethergate** was the 'lower way' through Dundee east to west, 'nether' coming from the Dutch *neder*, meaning 'lower' (as in the Low Counties or Netherlands), related to Old English *nithera* (and giving us the phrase 'nether regions').

* **Seagate** is the 'way' from the castle to the seafront, or more accurately, the River Tay.

EDINBURGH

* **Canongate**. Now part of the Royal Mile, this is the route the canons of Holyrood Abbey took into the town.

* **Cowgate**. The way along which cows were led to market in Edinburgh. Hibernian Football Club (Hibs) was founded by members of the congregation of St Patrick's Church on Cowgate, and the trophies won by the club are on display in the church.

* **Kirkgate**. The 'way to the kirk (church)', in this case the kirk in Leith.

* **West Port**. The street leading away from the West Port, the only gate in the western city walls. Here the actual gate is called a 'port' from the Latin *porta*, meaning 'entrance' and which also gives us 'portal' and '(sea)port'.

GLASGOW

* **Drygate** comes from the Gaelic *drui*, meaning 'sorcerer' or 'seer of the truth' and which also gives us 'druid' and hence a type of priest. So Drygate, which leads to the Necropolis and the cathedral, was the 'way of the priests'.

NORTH OF ENGLAND

ALNWICK, NORTHUMBERLAND

* **Bailiffgate**. The street where the duke's bailiffs had their offices.

* **Bondgate Within** and **Bondgate Without**. Alnwick Castle is the ancestral home of the Percys, Dukes of Northumberland, and Bondgate was the street along which the bondsmen who served the family in medieval times would pass in and out of the town. The part of the street that lies within the town walls is known as Bondgate Within while the part that lies outside the walls, where many of the bondsmen lived, is known as Bondgate Without.

* **Narrowgate**. Street that is, er, narrow.

* **Pottergate**. The street where potters had their workshops.

* **Walkergate**. Street down by the river where there was a fulling mill, where cloth was stretched and thickened (fulled) by pounding it with hands and feet. Fulling was also known as 'waulking' or 'walking', from the Scots Gaelic *waulk*, which means 'to full', as in the process of fulling. Cloth workers were hence known as 'waulkers' or 'walkers'.

DURHAM

* **Crossgate**. The street running from Durham city centre to Neville's Cross, half a mile west of the city. Originally a Saxon cross on a hilltop that marked the way for pilgrims travelling to Durham to pay their respects to the relics of St Cuthbert in Durham Cathedral, Neville's Cross was named in honour of Ralph Neville, who defeated a Scottish army under King David II there at the Battle of Neville's Cross in 1346. Also **Crossgate Peth**, the section of Crossgate leading down towards the river. 'Peth' is an archaic word for 'path', specifically a path leading down to a river.

* **Framwelgate**. From the Old English *fram*, meaning 'forth' or 'out of', and *wella*, meaning 'well' or 'spring'. Hence the street leading to where a spring gushes forth. Also **Framwelgate Waterside**, a street running along the river bank, and **Framwelgate Peth**, a street leading down to the river from the market. Also **Framwelgate Bridge**.

* **Gilesgate**. Like Gillygate in York (see page 50), this is a street leading to a church dedicated to St Giles.

* **Owengate**. A corruption of 'Ovengate', recalling the site of a long-disappeared medieval oven house, this is a curved side street leading up the hill to the cathedral.

YORK

In York 'gates' are streets while gateways are 'bars', because they bar or block the street. In total there are six 'bars' in York: four main ones in the city walls, used for tolls and defence; and two minor ones. York has perhaps more 'gates' than any other British city and their names can be very helpful in learning about the city's history and people, in particular its Roman and Viking past. **Petergate**, for instance, York's most prestigious and important street, runs along the route of the *via principalis* ('main street') of the original Roman fortress between the site of the city's two oldest gateways, from the *porta principalis dextra* or 'right gate' (Bootham Bar), as seen from the front of the camp headquarters, to the *porta principalis sinistra* or 'left gate' (which stood where King's Square is now). The name, given to it by the Vikings, comes from the Minster, which is dedicated to St Peter.

Here are some of the other more colourful York 'gates'.

* **Colliergate** is the street where coal was traded in the Middle Ages.

* **Coppergate** takes its name from the Viking *koppar*, meaning 'cup' or 'bowl', thus 'street of the cup makers'. Many wooden cups and bowls and similar items have been uncovered in the vicinity, suggesting that the street was home to a flourishing woodworking industry in medieval times.

* **Davygate**. Named after Davy Hall, home in the thirteenth century of David, the King's Lardiner or Larderer, who was responsible for keeping the king's larder supplied with meat, as well as game from the royal Forest of Galtres to the north of York. Davy Hall also served as courthouse and prison for the prosecution and punishment of forest poachers.

* **Feasegate**. Named after the Old Norse *fe-hus*, meaning 'cowhouse' or 'cattlepen' - in other words the street where cows were penned.

* **Fishergate** is the street where fishermen traded. Fishergate Bar, one of the two minor gateways in the city walls, opens on to it.

* **Fossgate**. Street leading to the River Foss.

* **Gillygate**. Street leading to a church (now gone) dedicated to St Giles.

* **Hungate**. Street where the hunting hounds were kept.

* **Micklegate**. From the Old Norse *mykla*, meaning 'great', this is the main street running through the part of Old York that lies west of the River Ouse. At the west end of the street is Micklegate Bar, York's southern gateway through which monarchs traditionally entered the city, hence the Great Gate across the Great Way. The severed heads of traitors were displayed on the gate, including those of Richard Plantagenet, 3rd Duke of York, father of Edward IV and Richard III, and Sir Henry 'Hotspur' Percy (after whom Tottenham Hotspur Football Club is named), supporter of Henry IV against Richard II.

* **Monkgate**. Street used by the monks of St Mary's Abbey. Monk Bar, a four-storey defensive gatehouse, intended as a self-contained fort, is one of the four main city gates.

* **Nessgate**. 'Ness' comes from an Old English word meaning 'promontory' (derived from the Old Norse *nes*, meaning 'nose'), and Nessgate leads to Clifford's Tower, all that remains of York Castle, which stands on a promontory that noses out between the rivers Ouse and Foss.

* **Skeldergate**. The city's main dockside street up until the

nineteenth century, Skeldergate derives either from the Old Norse *skjoldr*, meaning 'shield' (hence 'street of shield makers'), or the Old English *scylf*, meaning 'shelf', descriptive of the street as a flat piece of land between the river and the Bishophill area.

* **Spurriergate**. Street where the medieval makers of spurs traded.

* **Stonegate** follows the line of the Roman Via Pretoria, running from the river to the basilica at the centre of Roman York. This was York's first stone-paved street and survived into Viking times, hence the name, according to one theory. Another explanation is that this was the route used to convey the building stone for the Minster from the river after it had arrived from the quarries at Tadcaster.

* **Swinegate** is the street where swine or pigs were penned and where there were pork butchers. There is also a Swinegate in Hessle, Leeds, Shrewsbury and Grantham.

* **Walmgate**. Not an important thoroughfare in Roman York, this street was first recorded in Viking York as Walbagate, indicating that it takes its name from someone called 'Walba'. Walmgate Bar, one of the four main city gates, is the only town gate in England to retain its barbican or outer fortification.

SOUTH OF ENGLAND

CANTERBURY

Canterbury has a **Quenin Gate**, which rather splendidly comes from 'queen in'. This was the way taken by the sixth-century Queen Bertha, the first Saxon queen to be a Christian, between the city and her chapel, now the Church of St Martin.

COLCHESTER

* **Balkerne Gate**. The road from London (see 'Aldgate', opposite)
  entered Colchester through the Balkerne Gate, the biggest and
  oldest surviving Roman gate in Britain. No one seems to know
  where the name Balkerne comes from, but it may be from the Old to
  Middle English *balc*, which came to mean 'obstacle' and which has
  also given us 'balk' or 'baulk'.

* **Headgate**. Street named after the *hed* or 'main' gate into
  Colchester in medieval times.

* **Northgate**. Street leading along the northern walls.

* **Ryegate**, or Rivergate. From the Old English *rhee* or *rea*, meaning
  'bank of a river'. This street does indeed lead to the river.

LONDON

The City of London is one of the few cities in which the street names
ending in 'gate' derive from actual gateways in the former city walls.
The walled Roman city of Londinium had six gates that lasted in one
form or another until the end of the eighteenth century, by which
time they had all been demolished having become obstacles to traffic.
They are remembered, however, in the names of the streets that once
passed through them.

* **Aldersgate (Street)**. Street named after Ealdred's Gate, through
  which it passed. There is no record of which particular Ealdred
  was so honoured, but it may have been Ealdred the Archbishop
  of York, who crowned William the Conqueror in Westminster
  Abbey on Christmas Day in 1066. James I and VI entered the City
  for the first time through Aldersgate as king of both England and
  Scotland in 1603.

* **Aldgate**. From the Anglo-Saxon *eald*, meaning 'old', hence the Old Gate, this street led to what was perhaps the most important and widely used of London's Roman gates, for it stood over the road to the Roman capital of Camulodunum (Colchester). Between 1374 and 1385, Geoffrey Chaucer lived in a room above the gate. Queen Mary I entered the City for first time as queen through Aldgate in 1553.

* **Bishopsgate**. Street named after the Bishop's Gate, which takes its name from a Saxon bishop of London called Earconwald, who had the old Roman gate rebuilt in the seventh century. The Bull Inn, a coaching inn which stood on Bishopsgate from the early sixteenth century until 1866, was a favourite haunt of Thomas Hobson (*c*.1544-1631), the Cambridge horse owner who rented out his horses in strict rotation - the choice was the next horse in line or none at all, giving rise to the phrase 'Hobson's choice', meaning 'take it or leave it'. The great English stage actor Richard Burbage (*c*.1567-1619) performed plays at the Bull Inn before obtaining a licence from Elizabeth I to erect the original Globe Theatre on the south bank of the Thames. The Roman Ermine Street leading north through Spitalfields (Hospital Fields) to Lincoln and York started from Bishopsgate.

* **Cripplegate**. There is no street named after this particular gate, which was the northern entrance to the fort constructed by the Romans on the north bank of the Thames. The nearby church is dedicated to St Giles, the patron saint of cripples, which suggests that cripples came here to beg, hence the name. Elizabeth I entered the City for the first time as queen through Cripplegate. The gate gave access to the village of Islington where it joined with the street from Bishopsgate before heading north towards Lincoln and York as Ermine Street.

* **Ludgate (Hill)**. Street leading down the hill to the Roman Lud Gate, supposedly built by the ancient British king Lud. This was the City's westernmost gate and the name could plausibly have come from the Old English *hlidgeat*, meaning 'back gate'. The road through it led to a bridge across the River Fleet and on to Bath (Aque Sulis) and the south-west.

* **Moorgate**. Street named after the last of the gates to be built in the City walls, a Saxon postern gate called Moorgate, which led on to Moorfields, an area of marshland created by the damming of a stream that flowed by the City walls, the Walbrook. 'Moor' comes from the Old English *mor*, meaning 'marsh' or 'bog'. The poet John Keats was born on Moorgate in 1795, in the Swan and Hoop Inn where his father was an ostler.

* **Newgate (Street)**. Street named after the 'New Gate', so called because it was the last of the Roman gates to be built. Also taking its name from the gate was the notorious Newgate Prison, which stood on the site beside the gate for over seven hundred years. Public hangings took place outside the prison in Newgate Street.

4

SPECIFIC
STREET NAMES

So now we know why we name our streets and we know what names we give to different kinds of street. But once we have decided what type of street it is, how do we choose a specific name for it?

WAY

The names the Saxons gave to their streets are the oldest street names that survive. If a Roman paved road was a 'street', then one of the main unpaved tracks that criss-crossed England would be called a *weg* or 'way' (see page 12), such as the Ridgeway or the Icknield Way. Many of the less important unnamed ancient tracks survive to this day as footpaths, bridleways and other rights of way, and are sometimes known as 'green lanes'.

Here are some examples of Great Britain's prehistoric 'ways'.

FOSSE WAY

'Fosse' comes from the Latin *fossa*, meaning 'ditch', and it seems likely that the road began life as a prehistoric defensive ditch or causeway as, for some time after the Roman invasion in AD 43, it marked the western limit of the Roman Empire in Britain. The old 'way' was upgraded and paved by the Romans and became one of Britain's major Roman roads. It runs between Exeter in the south-west and Lincoln in the east.

ICKNIELD WAY

Running from the Peddars Way in Suffolk to the Ridgeway in Buckinghamshire, the Icknield Way is part of a network of ancient roadways that stretch from Norfolk to Wiltshire. It is named after the Celtic Iceni tribe, who used the road to travel west from their home territory in East Anglia.

PEDDARS WAY

Peddars Way is a prehistoric track running for forty-six miles from Suffolk to the north Norfolk coast. It was upgraded by the Romans and its name derives from the Latin *pedester*, meaning 'on foot'.

RIDGEWAY

'Ridge' is derived from the Anglo-Saxon *hrycg*, referring to the backbone or spine of a person or animal. The Saxons called Britain's oldest road the Ridgeway because, for the most part, it follows the ridge of the chalk hills of southern England. Part of a track that extended 250 miles from the Dorset coast to the Norfolk Wash, the Ridgeway stretches for eighty-five miles from Overton Hill, near the world's largest stone circle at Avebury in Wiltshire, to the distinctive Ivinghoe Beacon in the Chiltern Hills in Buckinghamshire. Used by cattle drovers, traders, soldiers, walkers, riders and travellers for over 5,000 years, since the days of the earliest settlers, it runs by many of England's most ancient treasures. These include Britain's oldest hill figure, the Uffington White Horse; Dragon Hill, where St George is believed to have slain the dragon; Wayland's Smithy, where King Arthur's sword Excalibur is said to have been forged; and the Iron Age hill forts of Barbury. Liddington, Uffington and Segsbury.

STREET

'Street', in the form of *straet* or *strate*, was what the Anglo-Saxons called the paved roads that the Romans had left behind (see page 12). The Romans did name their roads, after the various emperors, as a rule, but the names they gave to their roads in Britain have been lost, although it's more than possible that they were called after Roman governors of Britain who were in power when the roads were constructed. The first road the Romans built in Britain, for instance, which went from their landing place on the Kent coast to

London (now part of Watling Street), was most probably called the Via Claudia, in honour of the Emperor Claudius who led the Roman invasion of Britain in AD 43.

It was, however, the Anglo-Saxons who gave Britain's Roman roads the names by which we know them today. Here are some examples.

DERE STREET

Extending from York to the Roman Empire's northernmost boundary, the Antonine Wall in Scotland (Caledonia), Dere Street was so named as it ran through the Saxon kingdom of Deira, which in turn got its name from the River Derwent, derived from the old British word *derw* or *derwa*, meaning 'oak tree', thus 'river valley with oak trees'. Five or six sections of the A68 and other modern roads that follow the old route of the Roman road today bear the name Dere Street.

Settlements that lie on or near Roman roads often have one of the various words for 'street' as a prefix, such as *strat-*, *strait-* or *streat-*, including Streatham, 'homestead on the street', Stretton, 'settlement on the street', and Stretford or Stratford, 'ford on the street'.

ERMINE STREET

Ermine Street linked London with Lincoln (Lindum Colonia) and York (Eboracum) and roughly correlates to what became the Great North Road and then the A1. The name Ermine Street (Earniga Straete) is derived from the Anglo-Saxon Earnigas tribe, who occupied land in modern-day Cambridgeshire through which the road passed. In 1663 Ermine Street became Britain's first turnpike road whereby toll gates were set up to extract tolls from travellers along the road, which were then used for the road's upkeep. Britain's first stagecoach service ran between London and York along Ermine Street, and in the eighteenth and nineteenth centuries Ermine Street became Britain's busiest and most important turnpike road. There are fourteen Ermine Streets in Britain, almost all of them in eastern England near to the route of the original Roman road. There is an Ermine Street in Yeovil in Somerset, however, which may reflect the fact that another major Roman road, the Fosse Way (see page 57), runs close by through Yeovil.

STANE STREET

This ran from Chichester (Noviomagus Reginorum) to the Roman London Bridge across the Thames. 'Stane' is an old spelling of 'stone' and the name was often used to identify a paved Roman road.

THE STREET

There are over three hundred roads in Britain called The Street. Like High Street, the name The Street is usually given to the main street in a community, and in medieval times it would have been the only paved road in the town or village, with muddy unpaved tracks or paths leading off it. A good example can be found running through Castle Combe in Wiltshire. Castle Combe is many people's idea of the perfect English village - indeed, in 1962 it won the title of Prettiest Village and is often used as a picturesque filming location, most famously for the 1967 film *Doctor Dolittle*, starring Rex Harrison.

The village basically consists of one long street - The Street - which winds up through a deep wooded combe past rows of honey-coloured cottages, past the church, through the village square with its tiny market cross and past the Lamb Inn, so named for the Cotswold sheep whose wool made the village prosperous. **West Street** leads west from the market square to the manor house, now a hotel, along what would have been a simple dirt-track driveway, while further up the hill the narrow **School Lane**, now a private road but once a muddy footpath, leads to the old school house.

WATLING STREET

Originally known as Weacelinga Straet, then Watlingestrate, Watling Street runs from Dover (Dubris) to Wroxeter (Virocomium) via London (Londinium) and St Albans (Verulamium). It follows a route used by ancient Britons that took advantage of a ford across the Thames at Westminster and accords roughly with the route of the modern A2 south-east of London and the modern A5 north-west of the city. North of London the road passed through a settlement called Wætlingaceaster, near the modern St Albans, home of the Saxon Wætlingas people, and the name Watling Street is taken from them. Various sections of modern road along the historical route maintain the name Watling Street, in particular sections running through south-east London and a short stretch in the City of London.

Watling Street has played a significant role in Britain's history over the years. The Romans defeated Queen Boudicca on Watling Street in AD 60 or 61, and the road later became the boundary between King Alfred's Wessex and the territory ruled over by the Danes that was known as the Danelaw. Today Watling Street still forms much of the boundary between the counties of Leicestershire and Warwickshire, while the line the road takes through north-west London is sometimes used to define the boundary between west and north London.

CHRONOLOGY OF STREET NAMES

In Saxon and early medieval England, 'streets' were the paved ways, while other types of way were mostly simple grassy tracks. Village streets were given practical names drawn from nature - Hill, Oak, Water, or from prominent buildings - Church, Mill, Farm. In urban areas, streets were given names that reflected urban features and buildings - Gate, Market, Castle; professions and trades - Butcher, Baker, Corn, Cloth; their destination - London, York, Edinburgh, Bath; or their location within the town - East, West, South, North.

Later, in the Georgian and Victorian eras, as towns and cities expanded and as the number of streets multiplied, paving over countryside and obscuring natural features, it became necessary to think up more imaginative street names. Often they were taken from the landowners or builders who owned and developed the land on which the streets were laid out - **Portland Road**, **Harley Street**, **Grosvenor Square**. Royal names were popular, such as George or Victoria, as were the names of national heroes, such as Nelson or Wellington, or national events - Jubilee, Exhibition, Trafalgar. Then there were national statesmen, such as Gladstone, Lord Salisbury, Palmerston and Peel, or writers and poets, including Byron, Dickens and Tennyson, or local dignitaries, businessmen and philanthropists well regarded by their communities. All of these give us an insight into the events, history and cultural values, both local and national, of our towns and cities over the years.

Modern street names often reflect local celebrities (**John Lennon Drive** in Liverpool, for instance), political mores (**Sustainability Way** in Leyland, **Equality Road** in Birmingham) and, ironically, the natural features that the street may have replaced (Orchard Way, The Grove, Field Place).

In the next chapters we will look at some examples of all these different types of street names, beginning with streets named after natural features.

5

NATURAL
FEATURES

TREES, HILLS AND MEADOWS

The most common street name taken from nature is **Green Lane**, of which there are over a thousand. 'Green lane' is also commonly used as a general term for any unpaved country lane or track or byway where vegetation can gain a hold. A Green Lane that is most definitely no longer a green lane is **Green Lanes** in north London, which runs for six and a half miles between Newington Green and Winchmore Hill. So called because it was an ancient green way along which farmers drove their cattle into London, it is a good example of a street that no longer reflects its name.

Grove Road and **The Grove**, from the Old English *graf*, meaning 'small wood', are also among the fifty most common street names and they tend to be, or would like to give the impression that they are, upmarket residential streets.

There are many streets named after Britain's most common trees and plants, including Oak, Ash, Beech, Chestnut, Willow and Elm (the latter once numerous throughout England but tragically decimated by Dutch elm disease in the 1960s). There are also numerous Bush Streets, Water Lanes, River Streets, Brook Streets, Marsh Lanes, Bog Ends, Valley Roads, Hollow Lanes, Wood Lanes and Forest Roads.

Below are some famous examples.

BELMONT STREET, ABERDEEN

The name comes from the French for 'beautiful mountain' or 'beautiful hill' and the street was laid out in the eighteenth century on a hill overlooking the River Denburn.

BROADMEAD, BRISTOL

Now the main street of Bristol's shopping centre, Broadmead is one of the city's oldest streets, first recorded in 1383 as Brodemede, meaning 'broad meadow'.

CUMLODEN ROAD, NEWTON STEWART, DUMFRIES AND GALLOWAY

Cumloden comes from the Scots Gaelic words *cum*, meaning 'to hold' or 'to keep', and *lodan*, meaning 'marsh', hence a boggy marshland. As well as Cumloden Road, **Cumloden Mews**, **Court** and **House** all get their name from the village of Cumloden, where they are located. The area was given by Robert the Bruce to the Mackie of Larg, whose remarkable archery skills helped him triumph at the Battle of Glentrool in 1307.

ELM HILL, NORWICH

The elm trees after which Elm Hill is named were first planted in the sixteenth century but, alas, they are no longer there, having been struck down by Dutch elm disease in the 1970s. Fortunately, Elm Hill remains idyllic, a narrow, winding, cobbled street lined with early sixteenth-century, pastel-painted, timber-framed houses, and with a tiny sloping square at the top where the trees once stood. Mind you, in 1926 the street itself nearly went the way of the elm trees when Norwich council decided to demolish it, since it had become something of a slum, but they were persuaded instead to clean the area up and restore the buildings, and Elm Hill is now one of Norwich's most popular and recognisable landmarks. The street was first developed in the fifteenth century but was virtually destroyed by a fire in 1507, with only the Britons Arms, which stood slightly apart at the top of the hill, left standing. This glorious old building, which has one of Norwich's few remaining thatched roofs, dates back to 1347 and was originally built as a beguinage - a house for poor, single lay women who dedicated their lives to prayer and charity work. The steep gable of the Britons Arms is reminiscent of Flemish architecture and it is likely that this beguinage was founded, or at least influenced, by Norwich's large community of Flemish weavers who came to the town from the Low Countries where such beguinages were fairly common. It is, however, the only beguinage to be found anywhere in Britain.

Elm trees were, until the 1960s, the dominant tree in the English landscape, and hence there are many hundreds of streets of every kind across Britain with 'elm' in the name - Elm Grove, Elm Road, Elm Walk, Elm View and more - but I could only find one other Elm Hill, a modern housing estate in Warminster in Wiltshire.

FENCHURCH STREET, CITY OF LONDON
Laid out on the site of a church built where there was once a fen or marsh, the street gives its name to Fenchurch Street Station, the only railway terminus in the City.

FUNGLE ROAD, ABERDEENSHIRE
An ancient drovers' road passing through the Grampian Mountains between Glen Esk in Angus and Aboyne on Deeside in Aberdeenshire. Since the Scots Gaelic word for fungus is *fungas*, it would seem that this is a road along which fungus grew, the fungus probably in this case being mushrooms. So another name might be the Mushroom Road.

GOLD HILL, SHAFTESBURY, DORSET
'Last stop on round would be old Ma Peggotty's place. 'Twas like taking bread to the top of the world.' Back in 1973 these words turned Gold Hill into the most famous street in Britain. Described by John Hyams in *The Batsford Colour Book of Dorset* as 'one of the

most romantic sights in England', Gold Hill was chosen by a young film director called Ridley Scott as the perfect location for the Hovis 'Boy on a Bike' television advert, in which a boy is seen laboriously pushing his bike, laden with bread, up the hill to make a delivery, before freewheeling back down to the bakery. (I have long wondered if the boy made it safely to the bottom - Gold Hill is mighty steep and bumpy and he is last seen hurtling down the hill in an alarmingly reckless fashion.)

The idea was to promote the wholesomeness of the bread by evoking an atmosphere of a bucolic, pre-industrial, sepia-tinted northern England, appealing to our nostalgia for a simpler, rural past, and hence the boy wears a flat cap, the voiceover assumes a northern dialect and the music, Dvořák's *New World Symphony*, is played by a Lancashire colliery band.

It worked. Sales of Hovis bread boomed and the advert has regularly been voted Britain's favourite television commercial of all time. So effective was it in portraying the romantic north that it comes as something of a surprise to find out that Gold Hill is not actually in gritty Lancashire or Yorkshire but in that softest of soft south counties, Dorset.

Gold Hill today still presents an unchanging picture of idyllic rural England. No cars, no yellow lines or road signs or satellite dishes intrude. The steep, cobbled street descends between picturesque old thatched cottages and the buttressed fourteenth-century precinct walls of Shaftesbury Abbey, founded by Alfred the Great and burial place of King Edward the Martyr, said to have been murdered by his stepmother to clear the way for her son Ethelred the Unready. All against the luscious backdrop of the green and undulating Blackmore Vale. Gold Hill means 'hill of golden flowers', probably marigolds or daffodils, both of which flourish on the hill. Certainly the annual spring display of daffodils on the abbey terraces more than justifies the delightful name, although to many people across Britain, this iconic, enchanting street will always be Hovis Hill.

HURST STREET, BIRMINGHAM

From the Anglo-Saxon *hyrst*, meaning a wooded hill, this street rises up the hill from the River Rea. Birmingham's only remaining nineteenth-century back-to-back terraced houses are on Hurst Street. Built for industrial workers, the back-to-back style was eventually condemned and most were demolished. These picture-perfect examples are now run as a museum by the National Trust.

LITTLE BUSHEY LANE, BUSHEY, HERTFORDSHIRE

Bushey stands in an area that was once densely wooded and its name comes from *bysce*, the Old English word for a bush or thicket. Little Bushey Lane takes its name from the town through which it runs, while the 'little' is probably used in the archaic sense of 'lower'.

MEADOW WAY, OLD WINDSOR, BERKSHIRE

One of the many old 'King's' ways used by the king to get to Windsor Castle across the Thames water meadows.

NINE TREE HILL, BRISTOL

This residential road in Stokes Croft, a trendy part of Bristol, climbs steeply up from **Cheltenham Road**, the main road out of Bristol towards Cheltenham, and is named after nine elm trees that once stood on the hill. The trees were apparently burned down by vandals in the nineteenth century.

SAUCHIEHALL STREET, GLASGOW

Undoubtedly Glasgow's most famous thoroughfare and, at one and a half miles long, one of the city's longest streets, Sauchiehall Street gets its name from the Scots words *sauchie*, meaning 'willow', and *hauch* (pronounced 'haw'), meaning 'water meadow', hence 'the street through the willow-clad water meadows'. It began life as a country lane known as the Sauchie-haugh Road that ran west from St Mungo's Cathedral in Glasgow to the village of Partick through the willow-clad water meadows that lay between two hills, Blythswood Hill and Garnet Hill. In the 1800s Glasgow's wealthy merchants began to build themselves handsome villas on the western outskirts of the city near Partick, and the narrow, winding Saughie-haugh Road was straightened and made wider to provide easier access for the merchants travelling between their offices in the city centre and their new homes. Offices and shops were built along the route, turning the road into a street, and it was renamed Sauchiehall Street in the 1840s. It is the only Sauchiehall Street in the world.

The *sauchie* in Sauchiehall Street gives its name to the celebrated Willow Tea Rooms, opened in 1903 at 217 Sauchiehall Street by local businesswoman and temperance campaigner Catherine Cranston (1849-1934), as one of the first places in Glasgow where women could socialise outside the home. The tea rooms were designed in his own unique Art Nouveau style by the renowned Glasgow architect Charles Rennie Mackintosh, who used willow as his theme for the interior decoration. The Willow is the only one of the four tea rooms Mackintosh designed for Catherine Cranston to survive and has been restored to its original design by the Willow Tea Rooms Trust.

A slightly later Art Deco masterpiece, the Beresford Hotel, opened at 450 Sauchiehall Street in 1938 to accommodate visitors to the Empire Exhibition being held in Glasgow that year. At seven storeys high, it is regarded as Glasgow's first 'skyscraper' and is one of the finest Art Deco buildings in Glasgow. The following year, in 1939, a twenty-two-year-old John F. Kennedy gave his first-ever international speech at the Beresford, having been sent to Glasgow by his father Joseph Kennedy, then US Ambassador to Britain, to help the American survivors of the liner the *Athenia*, torpedoed by a German U-boat in the North Atlantic within hours of war being declared on 3 September 1939. Those passengers who were rescued were taken to Glasgow while the 117 passengers, including twenty-eight Americans, who did not survive, became the first civilian casualties of the Second World War. The Beresford is now divided into privately owned apartments.

But perhaps the most infamous building ever to stand on Sauchiehall Street was the Frank Matcham-designed Glasgow Empire, which opened in 1897 at No. 31 and became lovingly known as the 'place where English comics go to die'. Friday and Saturday night audiences made up of no-nonsense ship workers fresh out of the pubs would express their views about any act that didn't make them laugh by throwing bolts and rivets at the performers. Bob Monkhouse, Tommy Cooper, Bernie Winters and even Morecombe and Wise were all bombarded and jeered at the Glasgow Empire, while Des O'Connor only made it off the stage alive by pretending to faint so he could be rescued by the stage hands. The theatre finally closed its doors in 1963 and comedians all over England breathed a sigh of relief.

SMITHFIELD STREET, LONDON
A corruption of 'Smooth Field', this street leads to London's Smithfield Market, set up in medieval times on the flat and open area outside the City walls.

TINKERBUSH LANE, WANTAGE, OXFORDSHIRE
A tinker is an itinerant mender of kettles, pots and pans and this street name refers to a wood or thicket where a tinker lived. The author and Puritan preacher John Bunyan (1628-88) began life as a

tinker and was ever afterwards known as the 'Immortal Tinker'. He lived in Bedford, and for a short time in London, however (see page 175), not here, so he is not the tinker of Tinkerbush Lane.

WHITELADIES ROAD, BRISTOL

Bristol's longest and most famous street is named after a pub, the White Ladies Inn, shown on a map from 1746. The pub was itself named after White Ladies House, which was in turn named after a field of 'white ladies', or snowdrops.

RIVERS AND STREAMS

Virtually every village, town and city in Britain has at least one street named after the river or rivers that run through it. The longer and more significant the river, the more streets are named after it. Funnily enough, the most common river name for streets is Trent Road - there are more than fifty of them. There are over sixty Thames Streets and Roads combined and goodness knows how many Thames Views and Closes and Sides. There are some forty Severn Ways and Streets and some thirty Tyne Streets and Roads. Glasgow has its **Clyde Street**, Edinburgh its **Forth Street**, Dundee its **Tay Street** and Aberdeen its **Dee Street** and **Don Street**.

DEANSGATE, MANCHESTER

Manchester's oldest and longest city-centre street was a Roman road that led south from a ford over the River Medlock, past the Roman fort of Mamucium (also known as Mancunium) to the road to Chester (Deva). The Saxons called it Aldport, the Old (*ald*) Way (*port*) to Mamucium. It is now named Deansgate as it follows the route of the lost River Dene from its junction or 'gate' with the rivers Irk and Irwell near Manchester Cathedral.

FLEET STREET, LONDON

Named after the River Fleet, which rises on Hampstead Heath and joins the River Thames at **Blackfriars Bridge** - the bridge being named after the Dominican Friars who established a monastery here in the thirteenth century. They wore black habits and were hence known as the Black Friars. Fleet Street is a continuation of the main route between Westminster and the City of London and includes Temple Bar ('bar' meaning 'gate', as in York - see page 49), the main ceremonial entrance into the City. The monarch must stop here and request permission from the Lord Mayor to enter the City. In 1702 the world's first daily newspaper, the *Daily Courant*, began to be printed on Fleet Street and for much of the twentieth century the street was home to virtually all of the national daily papers, the *Express*, *Telegraph*, *Mail*, *Sun*, *Observer* and *Mirror* among them, until 'Fleet Street' become the generic term for the national press. The street's association with printing began way back in 1500 when Wynkyn de Worde, apprentice to Britain's first printer, William Caxton, at Westminster Abbey, set up shop just off Fleet Street so as to take advantage of the bookbinding and writing skills of the monks and clergy from nearby Blackfriars and St Paul's Cathedral.

INCHINNAN DRIVE, RENFREWSHIRE

Inchinnan Drive leads to the village of Inchinnan whose name is derived from *inch*, an anglicised version of the Scotch Gaelic word *innis*, meaning 'island', and St Inan, a ninth-century saint from Iona, thus 'the island of St Inan'. Inchinnan is surrounded on three sides by the River Clyde and the Black Cart and was very possibly an island in the ninth century.

SHAD THAMES, LONDON

One of London's iconic streets, Shad Thames runs between warehouses linked with overhead gantries on the south side of the

River Thames east of Tower Bridge. This was the largest area of warehouses in Victorian London, used to store a whole range of foodstuffs, including grain, tea, coffee, spices, dried fruits and sugar, earning it the nickname the 'Larder of London'. The landowners were originally the Knights of St John and the name, Shad Thames, is believed to be a corruption of St John at Thames, referring to a church that once stood at the end of the street. An alternative and equally plausible explanation for the name is that it comes from a type of herring called a 'shad', which could once be caught in the Thames and may have been landed and stored in the warehouses of Shad Thames.

TIB STREET AND TIB LANE, MANCHESTER

An extension of Oldham Road, the main road out of Manchester to Oldham, Tib Street and Tib Lane are named after the River Tib, a tributary of the River Medlock, which marked the eastern boundary of the Roman Mamucium and remained the boundary until the town began to expand in medieval times. There is a story that the river was named Tib by the Roman soldiers who thought it looked like a diminutive version of the River Tiber in Rome. Alternatively, it could come from the Latin *tubus*, meaning 'tube' or 'pipe'. The river now runs entirely underground – through a pipe.

PARKS, FIELDS AND ORCHARDS

Many streets are also named after what you might call managed natural features, such as Park, Orchard and Field. **Cherry Street** in Birmingham, for instance, used to run through the cherry orchards of the Priory of St Thomas. **Dangerfield Avenue** in Bristol is built on the site of a field called Danger Field. Why the field was called that is up for debate, but 'danger' comes from the Middle English *daunger*, meaning 'domination' or 'authority', derived in turn from the Latin *dominus*, meaning 'lord' or 'master', and hence it could have been a field owned by the local squire.

Park Avenue and **Park Lane** are both among the forty most common street names and tend to be used for upmarket streets - after all, it is always nice to be close to a park. (See also 'Avenue' on page 15.)

PARK LANE, LONDON

Prestigious enough to be the second most expensive property on the Monopoly board, Park Lane began life as a country lane running along the eastern side of Hyde Park. In the nineteenth century the views over the park attracted the wealthy, who built themselves large townhouses on the eastern side of the lane, such as the Duke of Westminster's Grosvenor House and the Holroyd family's Dorchester House. The Holroyd fortune came from building canals for bringing fresh water to London, such as the New River, opened in 1613, which takes water from the River Lea in Hertfordshire. Park Lane has become one of London's main north-south routes and the great mansions, including Grosvenor House and Dorchester House, have been replaced by hotels and luxury car showrooms, though penthouses on Park Lane are still much sought after.

6

PHYSICAL ATTRIBUTES, SHAPE, DESTINATION OR LOCATION

PHYSICAL ATTRIBUTES OR SHAPE

Many streets are named after their physical attributes or shape
- Broad, Long, Wet, Crooked, Bow; their destination - London,
Gloucester, York, Glasgow; or their location within the town - East,
North, West, South. Some are named after their age, whether Old,
as in **Old Street** or **Old Road**, or New - **New Street** and **New Road**
are among the top forty most common street names. The irony is, of
course, that they are usually among the oldest streets, but they must
have been new at some point. Here are some examples.

BOW STREET, LONDON

This was laid out in 1637 in the shape of a bow as a residential street
by Francis Russell, 4th Earl of Bedford. Notable residents in the
seventeenth and eighteenth centuries included Oliver Cromwell,
woodcarver Grinling Gibbons, novelist Henry Fielding, author of *Tom
Jones*, and the actor-manager David Garrick, the first actor to be
buried in Westminster Abbey. The street gave its name to Britain's
first police force, the Bow Street Runners, who operated out of Bow
Street Magistrates' Court. Initially a force of six men, the group was
founded in 1749 by Henry Fielding, a magistrate as well as a writer.
When the Metropolitan Police Service was established by Sir Robert
Peel (giving rise to the term 'bobbies') in 1829, the force opened one
of its first police stations in Bow Street. In 1861 a blue light was put
up outside every police station to identify it as such, complementing
the policeman's blue uniform, which had been carefully chosen as a
neutral colour in distinction to military red. Whenever Queen Victoria
attended the Royal Opera House, which had been rebuilt on Bow
Street in 1858 after a series of disastrous fires, she objected to the
blue light outside the Bow Street police station as it reminded her of

the blue room at Windsor Castle where her beloved husband Prince Albert had died. As a result, the blue light was replaced with a white one, making this the only police station in Britain to have a white light hanging outside.

BROAD STREET, BIRMINGHAM

Initially a pathway across fields, this was widened when Birmingham began to expand in the eighteenth century and became what at that time was the city's broadest street.

BROADWAY

Broadway is one of the oldest street names and is among the top thirty most common street names in Britain. It means exactly what it says, a broad way. You very often find Broadways in suburbia, usually shopping streets that are named after their suburb, such as **Ealing Broadway** and **Muswell Hill Broadway** in London. Broadway in Hale, Greater Manchester, is apparently the most expensive street outside London and the south-east, No. 5 in Britain, although it is incorrectly named since a 'way' is meant to be a public right of way, but this Broadway is both a private road and a no-through road, and even prohibited to horses! It really should be a Walk (see page 27).

CRUMLIN ROAD, BELFAST

This is the main road leading out of Belfast to the town of Crumlin, from the Irish *cromghlinn*, meaning 'crooked glen'.

DIAGON ALLEY

A play on the word 'diagonally', Diagon Alley appears in J. K. Rowling's *Harry Potter* stories as the main shopping street for wizards in London. There are no real-life Diagon Alleys but there is one **Diagonal Road**, just outside the little village of St Athan in the Vale of Glamorgan in South Wales. The road gets its name from a straight stretch in the middle that heads in a slightly different direction from the sections at either end of the road, forming a diagonal link between them.

FENKLE STREET, ALNWICK AND NEWCASTLE UPON TYNE

Fenkle is an Anglo-Saxon word in the Northumbrian dialect for a bend or a corner, and these two streets do, indeed, bend or curve.

FINKLE STREET, YORK

Finkle, like *fenkle*, means 'crooked', and this is a crooked 'snickelway' or alleyway in York (see page 38), formerly known as Mucky Pig Lane since it once led to the pig market.

MOISTY LANE, MARCHINGTON, STAFFORDSHIRE

Moisty Lane runs from the village of Marchington and along the flood plain of the River Dove and is therefore liable to flooding, although since it runs along higher ground above the meadows it is more likely to be frequently enveloped by mist rising from the river than flood water. 'Moisty' is probably a misspelling of 'misty', making this Misty Lane. There is also a lovely-sounding **Misty Meadows** in Cambridge.

NARROW STREET, LIMEHOUSE, LONDON

This street is named Narrow Street because it is, er, narrow.

NEW STREET, BIRMINGHAM

One of the oldest streets in Birmingham, 'Newestret' is first recorded in 1397, suggesting that it was considered new more than seven hundred years ago. It is believed that it was the new road between the market at the centre of Birmingham, where the Bull Ring is now, and the home of the de Birmingham family at Dudley Castle ten miles to the west. The street has more recently given its name to the city's main station, Birmingham New Street.

SINDERINS, DUNDEE

Named from the Scots word *sinder*, meaning 'to part' or 'to sunder', Sinderins is where the **Perth Road**, the main road to Perth, splits or sunders into two roads, with the Perth Road continuing east to pass south of the city centre, while **Hawkhill**, the road up 'the hill where hawks fly', goes east to the north of the city centre.

STEEP HILL, LINCOLN

Steep Hill in Lincoln happens to be exactly what it says on the tin - a steep hill. The fourth-steepest street in England, in fact, according to the Ordnance Survey, at 1 in 6 or 16.12 degrees. Steep Hill formed part of the Roman Ermine Street running up from the ford across the River Witham to the Roman fortress at the top of the cliff and then on through the third-century Newport Arch, the oldest arch still in use by traffic, to head north for the Humber along what is now the A15. Today Steep Hill links the **High Street** to **Castle Square** and the cathedral. Between the hill and the High Street is a short, narrow street called **The Strait**, from the Latin *strictus*, meaning 'drawn tight' or 'restricted', which indeed it is. At The Strait's junction with Steep Hill is the twelfth-century Jew's House, one of the oldest houses still occupied in Britain. Next to it is the equally ancient Jew's Court, both recalling medieval Lincoln's significant Jewish community. Further up is the Norman House, dating from 1170.

The steepest street in England is **Vale Street** in Bristol's aptly named Totterdown district, at 1 in 4 or 22 degrees, followed, at 1 in 6 or 17.5 degrees, by the **Old Wyche Road** in Malvern, Worcestershire, named after the Old English *wych*, meaning 'place of salt' (as in the salt-mining towns of Droitwich, Nantwich and Northwich), this being on an Iron Age salt route. In third place is **Blake Street** in Sheffield, named after nineteenth-century master cutler John Blake, with a gradient of 1 in 6 or 16.6 degrees, and in fifth position is **Gold Hill** in Dorset (see page 67), at 1 in 6 or 16.09 degrees.

STRAIGHT ROAD, OLD WINDSOR, BERKSHIRE

Straight Road is so named, spookily enough, because it is a straight road. Just over a mile long, it was cut in 1816 to replace a number of winding lanes that meandered through the Thames water meadows to Windsor and were frequently flooded. There are seventeen Straight Roads, five roads called **Straight Mile** and one **Straight Bit**, in Flackwell Heath in Buckinghamshire, which is well named for it is only a bit straight and has quite a few kinks in it.

DESTINATION

The most prolific example of a street named after the place it leads to is **London Road**, the seventh- or eighth-most common street name in Britain. This is no doubt because, being the capital, all roads lead to London. Next comes **Manchester Road**, then **York Road**, followed, surprisingly, by **Chester Road**, **Richmond Road**, presumably because there are two important places called Richmond, one in London and one in North Yorkshire, and **Windsor Road**. I can only assume that Windsor is here because the name refers to the Royal House of Windsor as well as the town. What these featured towns all have in common is that they are either very old or very central, with roads passing through them in all directions.

In Scotland, the most common destination street name is **Perth Road** - again because it is central. Dundee has a Perth Road and an **Arbroath Road**. **Edinburgh Road** in Glasgow leads to Edinburgh while the **Glasgow Road** in Edinburgh leads to . . . Glasgow.

EDGBASTON STREET, BIRMINGHAM

One of the first roads in Birmingham to be paved. Edgbaston was originally a manor house recorded in the Domesday Book as Celboldestone or Egebaldestone, meaning the *tun* or 'place' of

Celbold or Egebalde. Edgbaston is home to Birmingham Botanical Gardens and to the two towers that inspired J. R. R. Tolkien's *The Two Towers*, the second volume of *The Lord of the Rings*, the eighteenth-century Perrott's Folly and the Victorian Edgbaston Waterworks Tower. Tolkien grew up in Edgbaston, which is also host to a Test cricket venue and the oldest tennis club in the world still operating, the Edgbaston Archery and Lawn Tennis Society, founded in 1860. The first-ever game of lawn tennis was played in Edgbaston in 1859, in the garden of a house called Fairlawn, between Spanish-born Augurio Perera and Major Harry Gem, who was experimenting with a way to play a racquet game outdoors. He originally called the game Sphairistike, after *sphairos*, the Greek word for 'ball', but his friend, the future prime minister Arthur Balfour, suggested 'lawn tennis' might be a better name.

Also in Birmingham, **Bristol Street** was the old turnpike road to Bristol, **Dudley Street** the old road to Dudley and **Pershore Street** led to the abbey at Pershore. Bristol, meanwhile, has the **Gloucester Road**, a **Cheltenham Road** and a **Bath Road**.

LIVERPOOL ROAD, MANCHESTER

The main road out of Manchester to Liverpool gives its name to the world's oldest surviving inter-city railway terminus, Manchester's Liverpool Road station, which opened in 1830 and was designed by the 'Father of the Railways', George Stephenson. After a spell serving as the set of *Coronation Street* (see page 143), it now houses part of the Museum of Science and Industry in Manchester.

OLD KENT ROAD

A good example of a street named after the place it leads to or from, in this case Kent, today the Old Kent Road forms the first section of the modern A2, beginning at the **Bricklayers Arms** roundabout in

Walworth, south London (named after a seventeenth-century pub that stood on the spot), and running south-east to New Cross. The road from Kent is one of Britain's oldest roads, originally an ancient Celtic trackway and the first road to be paved by the Romans when they landed in Britain, under the command of the Emperor Claudius, in AD 43. It was one of the most important roads in Roman Britain, linking London to Richborough (Rutupiae) on the Kent coast, which is where the Romans had established a beachhead for their invasion force and which became the Romans' principal port, serving traffic between Britannia and Rome itself. The Bricklayers Arms roundabout marks where the road met Stane Street, the Roman road from Chichester, before both roads turned north to cross the Thames at London Bridge.

The Anglo-Saxons called the road Watling Street, a name it retains to this day in some parts as it wends its way through south-east London.

The pilgrims in Chaucer's *Canterbury Tales* rode along 'Kent Street' on their way from London to Canterbury, stopping at a small stream that crossed what was then a country road in order to allow their horses to drink. While they waited, the pilgrims drew lots to see who should be first to tell a tale - the knight won the honour. Years later, a tavern was put up by the stream so that riders could refresh themselves as well as their horses, and the spot became known as St Thomas-a-Watering. On 23 November 1415, the Bishop of London and other London dignitaries welcomed the victorious Henry V and his men back from the Battle of Agincourt at St Thomas-a-Watering. In later years it became a place of execution, particularly for those who crossed Henry VIII, and nearby **Penry Street** remembers the Welsh Protestant martyr John Penry who was hanged there in 1593. In 1660, on his birthday, 29 May, Charles II rode by on his way into London from Dover, where he had landed on his restoration to the throne, 'with a triumph of about 20,000 horse and foote, brandishing their swords and shouting with inexpressible joy; the wayes strew'd with flowers, the bells ringing, the streets hung with tapestrie, fountaines running with wine', as the diarist John Evelyn tells us.

Incidentally, **Rolls Road** just off the Old Kent Road recalls the Rolls family, ancestors of Charles Stewart Rolls of Rolls-Royce fame who developed the land they owned there during the eighteenth century. The White House at No. 155, which served as the headquarters of the estate, is all that remains; buildings including schools and a library were destroyed by bombing raids during the Second World War.

OXFORD STREET, LONDON

The road to Oxford from London follows the route of a Roman road, the Via Trinobantina, which ran from Hampshire to Suffolk through London and has long been one of the major routes west out of the capital. In medieval times, the street was the route that prisoners took from Newgate Prison to the gallows at Tyburn, where Marble Arch is now. It began to develop as a shopping street in the mid-nineteenth century, with John Lewis being the first of the major stores to open in 1864, followed by Selfridges in 1909 (run on the motto 'the customer is always right'), and by the mid-twentieth century, Oxford Street was Europe's busiest shopping street, which it remains today. As Napoleon did point out, England is 'a nation of shopkeepers'.

PALATINE ROAD, WITHINGTON, MANCHESTER

Originally a turnpike called the Northendon New Road, this street was renamed in 1887 at the request of the Post Office. The name comes from the fact that the road runs between the county palatines of Lancashire and Cheshire. Palatine comes from the Latin *palatinus*, meaning 'relating to the palatium or palace', and these palatine counties were ruled over by a count or earl on behalf of the monarch, enjoying a certain amount of autonomy.

SCOTLAND ROAD, LIVERPOOL

Affectionately known as Scottie Road, this street was laid out in the eighteenth century as a turnpike, running north from the city centre towards Preston, and quickly became the beginning of the stagecoach route from Liverpool to Scotland. Actor Tom Baker (born in 1934), the fourth Doctor in *Doctor Who*, was born on Scotland Road, and singer Cilla Black (1943-2015) grew up on Scotland Road in a small flat above a barber's shop.

LOCATION

Most towns have at least one street that gets its name from its location within the town: **East Street** will be east of the town centre, **South Street** south of the town centre, and so on. Streets can also be named for the direction of travel, hence the Great North Road, which ran between England and Scotland and whose route is traced today by the A1, is a road that heads north (from London). For some reason, there are many more West Streets and Roads than East Streets and Roads and many more North Streets and Roads than South Streets and Roads. It could be that because the biggest city, London, is in the south-east of Britain, there are simply more roads heading north and west from London than south and east.

7

TRADES
AND TRADERS

Many of our more ancient streets were named after the type of activity or trade that was carried out on the street, or in some cases where certain types of trader lived.

The City of London, as Britain's biggest and busiest medieval marketplace, provides us with some splendid examples of such street names. It is also one of Britain's oldest places of business - so old, in fact, that it has no 'roads', since its streets were named before the term 'road' entered the language as an alternative to the general term 'way'. It was William Shakespeare who was first to use the word 'road' with anything like the same meaning it has today (that we know of), although he uses it only three or four times in his plays. In *Henry VIII* (Act 4, Scene 2), for instance, Katherine of Aragon's gentleman usher Griffith says of Cardinal Wolsey, 'At last, with easy roads, he came to Leicester', and in *As You Like It* (Act 2, Scene 3), Adam, the faithful family retainer, tries to prevent Orlando from entering the family home where Orlando's brother is plotting to murder him, to which Orlando replies, 'What, wouldst thou have me go and beg my food, / Or with a base and boist'rous sword enforce / A thievish living on the common road?'

CITY OF LONDON STREETS

BREAD STREET

This was where bakers plied their trade. Edward I decreed that all the bakers of London and surrounding areas were not allowed to sell bread from their own bakeries but only on Bread Street, presumably so that he could help himself to a goodly portion of the takings. Perhaps that's why money is known as 'bread'?

CAMOMILE STREET

This follows the line of the old Roman wall and is named for the wild camomile flowers that used to grow among the ruins.

CHEAPSIDE

London's original 'high street', Cheapside was the site of London's main food market, its name derived from the Old English *ceap*, meaning 'market'. It also gives us the word 'cheap', as in inexpensive, for the market was where you could bargain to get things at a low price. The streets to either side of Cheapside are named for the produce you could buy there.

COCK LANE

Cock Lane - stop laughing at the back there - is where cockerels were bred and sold for cock fighting, and in the fourteenth century it was, either coincidentally or naturally, depending on your turn of mind, the only place in the City of London where prostitutes were allowed to ply their trade. **Stew Lane**, further east down by the river, was where prostitutes would embark on boats to cross the river on their way to the 'stews' or brothels on the South Bank.

CORNHILL

Cornhill reaches the highest point in the City and was the site of Londinium's Roman basilica, but gets its current name from the medieval grain market that occupied the eastern end of the street. Similarly, **Corn Street** in Bristol, one of the city's earliest streets, is where corn was known to have been traded as far back as the thirteenth century.

FISH STREET HILL

This was originally the main road leading up to London Bridge and is where fish could legally be sold in the city outside Billingsgate

Market. The Fishmongers Hall was set up on the street in 1310 and remains in situ, the present building being the fourth one on the site. Inside you can find the dagger with which the fishmonger and Lord Mayor of London, William Walworth, killed Wat Tyler, the leader of the Peasants' Revolt, in 1381. Shrewsbury has a **Fish Street**.

GARLICK HILL

Garlick Hill led up to the markets of Cheapside from the dock where garlic was landed, which was known as Garlickhythe, *hythe* being a landing place.

HERBAL HILL

This street name recalls the sixteenth-century herbalist John Gerard, who had a garden somewhere near Fleet Street and wrote the first-ever book of herbs.

HONEY LANE

This was where beekeepers lived and where their honey was sold. Honey Lane Market was London's smallest market.

LIME STREET

Lime Street was where lime burners lived and traded in lime, a chemical substance derived from limestone. The lime was actually burned in lime kilns located east of the city in the district now known as Limehouse.

MILK STREET

This was where milk was sold and also where the milking cows were kept. Sir Thomas More was born on Milk Street in 1478 and the cookbook pioneer Mrs Beeton lived on the street as a child. Shrewsbury also has a Milk Street, while Exeter, whose Milk Street has, alas, disappeared, can instead boast a **Waterbeer Street**, or 'street of the water bearers', from the Old English *waterbere.*

POULTRY

The eastern extension of Cheapside, Poultry was the home of London's poulterers. There used to be an alleyway leading off it called **Scalding Alley**, the site of a Scalding House or Scalding Wicke, where freshly slaughtered poultry would be scalded to loosen the feathers before plucking.

PUDDING LANE

This is famous as the location of the baker's shop where the Great Fire of London started on 2 September 1666. Being something of a connoisseur of puddings, I have always been rather attracted to Pudding Lane, picturing all the glorious treacle and steak and kidney puddings that must have been cooked in the various premises I imagined lining the street. Imagine my distress on learning that the word 'pudding' is derived from the Latin *botellus*, via the Old French *boudin*, meaning a sausage made from an animal's guts and entrails. Pudding Lane, it turns out, was the route by which the rejected guts and entrails of animals sold in the medieval meat market on **Eastcheap** (named, like Cheapside, from the Old English *ceap*, meaning 'market', and 'East' to differentiate it from the West Market, as Cheapside used to be known) were brought down to the Thames to be loaded on to dung barges.

Apparently an eccentric Puritan minister of the time blamed the Great Fire of London on gluttony, since it began in Pudding Lane and ended at **Pie Corner** (named after an inn called the Magpie which stood nearby) at the junction of Cock Lane and **Giltspur Street** near Smithfield Market. A gold-painted statue of a distinctly chubby boy stands in a niche in the wall of the building on the corner, with an inscription below it which says: 'This Boy is in Memmory Put up for the late FIRE of LONDON Occasion'd by the Sin of Gluttony 1666.' Giltspur Street was originally called Knightrider Street because in medieval times knights would ride this way to the Smithfield tournaments. Some of the participants would replace their spurs with gilded ones made in premises on the street, hence it eventually became Giltspur Street. 'Spur', by the way, comes from the Old English *spura*, meaning 'to kick or strike with the foot'. There is another Knightrider Street by St Paul's Cathedral, running off **Addle Hill**, which itself comes from the Old Saxon *adel*, meaning 'noble' (in turn derived from *aðel*, pronounced 'athel' as in 'atheling', an Anglo-Saxon prince eligible for kingship), so clearly this was an area frequented by noble knights. Or it could just mean 'addle', of course, in the archaic sense of 'rotten', as derived from the Old English *adela*, referring to liquid manure. Bearing in mind how close we are to the stinking entrails of Pudding Lane, this seems entirely plausible.

SAFFRON HILL

Saffron Hill near Clerkenwell recalls the saffron crocuses that grew abundantly in the garden of the Bishop of Ely's palace that stood here. Saffron, obtained from the dried 'threads' (stigmas and styles) of the flowers, was one of the most widely used spices in medieval England.

THREADNEEDLE STREET

This takes its name from the needle and thread of the Merchant Taylors' Company whose hall is still situated in the street. The street is also home to the Bank of England, which is known colloquially as 'The Old Lady of Threadneedle Street'. The name comes from a 1797 political cartoon by James Gillray, in which a lady sitting on a chest marked 'Bank of England' is being ravaged by prime minister William Pitt the Younger (see page 127). The cartoon refers to Pitt's Bank Restriction Act, whereby the bank suspended redemption of notes for gold and began paying out in paper money rather than coins.

VINE STREET

Vine Street is named after the Vine Tavern that stood here in the eighteenth century. The tavern in turn took its name from a Roman vineyard that stood on the site.

WINE OFFICE COURT

This was where licences for selling wine were issued. You can now find there the entrance to one of London's most famous pubs, Ye Olde Cheshire Cheese, patronised by the likes of Samuel Johnson, Charles Dickens, Sir Arthur Conan Doyle, Winston Churchill and P. G. Wodehouse. **Peterborough Court** next door recalls that this was the site of the Bishop of Peterborough's London home, which had huge wine cellars that are now used by the pub. Nearby **Carmelite Street** and **Whitefriars Street** run along the site of a vanished thirteenth-century Carmelite priory - Carmelites were known as White Friars after the colour of their robes.

WORMWOOD STREET

A street that follows the line of the old Roman wall and is named for the wild wormwood plants that used to grow among the ruins. Wormwood has medicinal properties and is also used for flavouring wines and other alcoholic drinks such as bitters and vermouth. In eighteenth-century England it was sometimes used instead of hops for brewing beer.

STREETS IN LONDON AND FURTHER AFIELD

Other common street names derived from trades are Blacksmiths Lane, Ironmongers Row, Cartwrights Lane, Wheelwrights Row and Glovers Lane.

* **Ropemaker Street** in Finsbury, London, for instance, is the street where ropes were made and **Sugar Loaf Walk** in Bethnal Green takes its name for the sugar loaf sign that grocers would put outside their shop and sits on the site of an old sugar refinery. **Brewhouse Yard** in Clerkenwell stands on the site of the Cannon Brewery, founded in 1720, which was taken over by Taylor Walker and then Ind Coope, eventually becoming part of Allied Breweries.

* **Cloth Fair** in Smithfield was named for the annual Bartholomew Fair held at Smithfield for seven hundred years. This was England's most important cloth fair and cloth merchants travelled there from all over Europe.

* Other streets named for the cloth trade are **Lister Gate** in Nottingham, which was once Dyers Street, *lytster* being another word for a dyer, **Drapers Lane** in Leominster and the long-gone Tenter Close in Coventry, where cloth was 'tented' or stretched. Also **Needless Alley** in Birmingham. A local humorous saying tells us that 'there's only one alley in Birmingham and it's needless'. The name, however, is a corruption of 'Needlers', reflecting how there were needleworkers plying their trade in the alley as recently as the 1970s.

DOCKS

Down by the docks in London are a number of streets named after the produce landed and stored there.

Artichoke Hill is named after a pub that stood there, the pub itself being named after the vegetable, which was unloaded and stored in nearby warehouses. The globe artichoke first arrived in England in the sixteenth century and became a great favourite of Henry VIII. **Cinnamon Street** and **Cinnamon Wharf** near St Katherine's Dock was where cinnamon was offloaded and traded. Down by the old East India Dock at Canning Town, where many herbs and spices were offloaded and stored, we can find **Clove Crescent**, **Coriander Avenue**, **Nutmeg Lane**, **Oregano Drive**, **Rosemary Drive** and **Sorrel Lane**. Albeit not by the docks, an actual **Spicer Street** - from the French *épicier*, meaning a grocer, or seller of spices - may be found in St Albans, indicating that it was the street of the grocers.

BRICKYARDS AND POTTERIES

Brick Lane in east London was originally a winding country lane called Whitechapel Lane, its current name deriving from the brickyards that sprang up in the sixteenth century when brick earth deposits were discovered in the area. Brick Lane has been home to many different immigrant communities over time, including French Huguenots, the Irish, Jews and now Bangladeshis, who have made the street famous for its cuisine - in fact, it has the highest concentration of curry houses in Britain. There is a **Brick Street** running off Piccadilly in London W1 that recalls an old brick kiln that once stood there.

In **Pottery Lane** in Notting Hill, a lone bottle kiln at the top of the lane is all that remains of the potteries and brickfields that flourished here in the nineteenth century.

MARKETS AND FAIRS

Most British towns and cities have a market near the town centre, as indicated by street names such as **Market Street**, of which there are some 370 and Market Place (some 270), with goodness knows how many Market Squares, Ends, Crosses, Lanes, Views and more. King's Lynn in Norfolk has a **Tuesday Market Place** and a **Saturday Market Place**. The City of London has no Market Streets since it uses the old word 'cheap' instead, as found occasionally elsewhere.

Market Place in Salisbury was, in 1357, known as Chepyngplace. Canterbury has a **Wincheap**, from the Old English *waegnceap*, meaning 'wagon market'.

While many places, such as Manchester, have a Market Street, some towns name streets after specific markets: Aberdeen has **Mealmarket Street**; Glasgow has the **Saltmarket**; Dartmouth in Devon has a **Butterwalk**; and Ipswich has a **Buttermarket**, as does Canterbury in the square outside the cathedral, where butter, cheese and other dairy products were sold. It used to be called the Bullstake and was the place where bulls were tied up to a stake to be baited by dogs before being slaughtered - it was thought that bull-baiting, apart from being good sport, made the meat more tender. In Birmingham, bulls were led along **Bull Street** to a field in the marketplace where they were tied to rings for baiting - hence the name of the Bull Ring shopping centre.

Also in Birmingham is **Horsefair**, where the city's horse fair was located, though it ceased trading in 1912. **Pinfold Street**, from the Old English *pundfald*, meaning an enclosure for stray animals, is on the site of the old animal pound from where the owners could collect their animals after payment of a fine. **Livery Street**, meanwhile, named for the Swann's Riding Academy which stood on the site in the eighteenth century, is thought to be the longest street in Birmingham and gave rise to a local expression, 'a face as long as Livery Street', meaning to look miserable.

BUTCHERS

Another street name missing from the City of London is anything to do with butchers or butchery and this is because the cattle market was outside the City walls in Smithfield. Canterbury has a **Butchery Lane**, while Banbury, Barnstaple and Shrewsbury all have a **Butchers Row** and Edinburgh has its **Fleshmarket Close**. But the oldest and most colourful name for streets associated with butchery is 'shambles' and the most famous of these is **Shambles** in York.

The name Shambles or The Shambles denotes a street or a collection of streets where butchers slaughtered their cattle and sold their meat. The word is a medieval term derived from the Anglo-Saxon *shammel*, meaning 'stall' or 'shelf', and refers to the shelves on which the butchers displayed their cuts of meat. Several towns in Britain - including Guildford, Bradford-on-Avon, Worcester, Sevenoaks, Manchester, Chesterfield, Whitby and Chippenham - have a Shambles, usually found in the centre of town near the marketplace, but York's Shambles, originally The Great Flesh Shambles, is undoubtedly the most famous example.

It is the best-preserved medieval street in Britain, a narrow, cobbled thoroughfare lined with fourteenth-century timber-framed buildings with overhanging gables that almost touch each other, designed that way to provide shade for the meat. Many of the shops retain their shelves and still have the hooks and rails for hanging the meat above the shop window, while the raised pavements on either side allowed the butchers to wash the blood and gore away into the main street. In medieval times, the Shambles would have been a scene of blood-drenched mayhem and disorder and the term has evolved into its modern meaning of 'chaotic' or 'a mess'. York's Shambles is thought to be the inspiration for Diagon Alley in the *Harry Potter* series (see page 78).

Manchester has a **Shambles Square** (rebuilt and moved to near the cathedral after the IRA bombing of 1996). Oxford has a **Beef Lane**, the lane where beef was sold. It no longer contains any butcher's shops, however, and has been largely transformed into the north quad of Pembroke College.

FARMS, MILLS AND QUARRIES

* **Blossom Street**, York. There is no point in strolling down Blossom Street in the springtime hoping to see the cherry blossoms, for this was in fact the street where 'ploughswains', or ploughmen, lived and where ploughs were serviced and repaired. In a clear case of Chinese whispers, this street was originally called Ploughswaingate, which evolved into Ploxwangate, then Blossomgate and finally Blossom Street.

* **Millers Lane**, Outwood, Surrey. Named for the millers of England's oldest working post mill, the earliest European type of windmill, built on Outwood Common in 1665. It used to be one of a pair, the Cat and the Kitten, but the Kitten, a smock mill, collapsed in 1960. In 1666, the year after it was built, the millers climbed to the top floor of the Cat to watch the Great Fire of London.

* **Pork Lane**, Great Holland, Essex. Not another reference to a butcher (see page 95), but a road that runs through or by a pig farm.

* **Quarryheads Lane**, Durham. This is where the sandstone used to build Durham Cathedral was quarried.

* **Stationers Place**, Hemel Hempstead. Since the eighteenth century, Hemel Hempstead has been a centre of the paper and stationery industry. Stationers Place is the home of one of the world's first large-scale paper mills, the Apsley Paper Mill, founded in 1774 by stationer John Dickinson, who went on to invent a ground-breaking mechanised paper-making process. John Dickinson & Co. Ltd later took over Millington & Sons, producers of the famous Basildon Bond writing paper, which is named after Basildon Park, the country house in Berkshire where the company directors were

staying while they were thinking of what to call their new brand. The nearby Frogmore Paper Mill is the site of the first continuous paper-making machine in the world.

OVERSEAS TRADE

* **Baltic Street**, Dundee. A street recalling Dundee's trade with Riga on the Baltic Sea, the chief source of flax and hemp. **Whale Lane** and **Baffin Street** (after Baffin Bay in Canada) are named in memory of Dundee's whaling industry and **Candle Lane** and **Soapwork Lane** recall by-products of whaling.

* **Dantzic Street**, Manchester. Referring to an anglicised version of the Polish city of Danzig, now Gdansk, which reflects Manchester's trading links with the countries of the Baltic Sea.

* **Shiprow**, Aberdeen. One of Aberdeen's oldest streets, Shiprow was laid out in the thirteenth century to give passage up from the harbour to the castle. Aberdeen also has **Sugarhouse Lane** and **Virginia Street**, both named in the eighteenth century when Aberdeen was expanding its trade with Virginia in America.

8

DIFFERENT BUILDINGS AND OTHER STRUCTURES

In Saxon and medieval times, most communities were villages and hence older street names often refer to a type of building, usually one of the more important buildings, in the village. Those most commonly referred to in street names are Church, Park, Manor, Grange and Mill, with Chapel, Farm and Hall slightly further down the list, which all makes sense since every village has at least one of these types of building. Names based on structures such as Bridge, Cross, Spring or Well might also be used. There are over 500 Bridge Streets and 250 Bridge Roads. St Columb Major in Cornwall is the only place in Britain to have a street called simply **Bridge** - the old main road through the village is not a bridge itself but it does approach a bridge. Truro in Cornwall has a **Bridge Street**, named for a new bridge erected in 1775 over the River Truro.

Abbey, Priory, Friary, Nunnery and Convent are more prevalent as street names in larger communities, since towns naturally grew up around such establishments. As towns tended to have more than one church, it became necessary to distinguish between them, so the street names came to reflect a particular church, such as the old church (Old Church Road), the church with the white walls (Whitchurch Street) or a church devoted to a particular saint, giving rise to St Mary's Road or St Peter's Street.

During the eighteenth century, Britain became rapidly industrialised and new types of structure began to spring up, such as canals and quays and docks, and new types of buildings, such as factories and stations. Indeed, as we have already touched upon, **Station Road** is among the five most common street names (see page 15), reflecting the rapid rise of the railways in the nineteenth century.

CHURCHES AND RELIGIOUS HOUSES

ABBEY ROAD, ST JOHN'S WOOD, LONDON

Abbey Road gives its name to the most famous recording studios in the world and in so doing has itself become one of the most famous roads in the world. The world's first purpose-built recording studio opened in 1931 as the Gramophone Company Studios with a performance of 'Land of Hope and Glory' conducted by Sir Edward Elgar. It later became the EMI Recording Studios. In the 1960s the Beatles recorded 190 of their 210 songs there and called their 1969 album *Abbey Road* in honour of the road on which the studios stand. The following year, the studios was renamed Abbey Road Studios in honour of the album. The album cover featuring the four Beatles walking across the Abbey Road zebra crossing has become iconic and has made Abbey Road recognised around the world. The road was formerly a track leading to Kilburn Abbey, established in 1128 for three pious ladies-in-waiting of Queen Matilda of Scotland, first wife of Henry I. Hence Abbey Road. Across the road from the studios is the Abbey Road Baptist Church, where the Abbey Road Building Society was founded in 1874. It went on to become the Abbey National.

AUSTIN FRIARS, LONDON

Named after the medieval priory of Austin Friars that stood here.

CRUTCHED FRIARS, LONDON

This street derives its unusual name from the House of the Crutched Friars or Friars of the Holy Cross, which stood on the site from 1249 until the dissolution of the monasteries in 1539. 'Crutched' comes from the Latin word *crux*, meaning 'cross'. Known for carrying a staff surmounted by a crucifix, the monks were also referred to as the 'Crouched' or 'Crosiered' Friars. There are no other streets called Crutched Friars in Britain, but there is one **Crutch Furlong** in Berinsfield in Oxfordshire, three streets called **Crutch Lane** in the Midlands, and three called **Crutches Lane**, two in Kent and one in Beaconsfield, all of them likely to be on the site of monastic houses associated with the Holy Cross.

MARYLEBONE HIGH STREET AND MARYLEBONE ROAD, LONDON

Now a built-up area of offices, shops, hotels and apartment blocks, Marylebone, before the eighteenth century, was a small country village that took its name from the church of St Mary-le-Bourne or St Mary on the Bourne, 'bourne' meaning a stream, in this case the River Tyburn, or Ty bourne.

The present St Marylebone Church, which is the second church to stand on the site, is of classical design and was built by Thomas Hardwick in 1817. It quickly became a fashionable church. Lord Byron was christened here in 1778, as was Admiral Nelson's daughter Horatia by his lover Lady Emma Hamilton, in 1803. Ironically, Sir William Hamilton had married the then Emma Hart in the same church in 1791. The poet Robert Browning married Elizabeth Barrett in the church in 1746. In 1809 the 3rd Duke of Portland, twice prime minister, was buried in the churchyard, which has since been made into a public garden.

Marylebone High Street developed as the main street of the village when St Marylebone Church was opened at its northern end in 1400. Today it retains a village atmosphere and is lined with boutique shops and restaurants. Marylebone Road was laid out in 1756 as the western section of London's first bypass, the New Road, which ran from Marylebone to the Angel, Islington, forming London's then northern boundary. The New Road was renamed in 1857 as Marylebone Road, Euston Road and Pentonville Road.

MASSHOUSE CIRCUS, BIRMINGHAM

Large, elevated roundabout built on the site of the Mass House of St Mary Magdalen and St Francis. 'Mass House' was another name for a Roman Catholic church.

MOSES STREET, LIVERPOOL

There is an area of Dingle in Liverpool known as The Holy Land in which a cluster of Victorian terraced streets, while not named after churches as such, are instead called after characters in the Bible, hence **Isaac Street**, **David Street** and **Jacob Street**. Belfast also has a 'Holy Land', created by builder James Rea, who had just returned from a trip to the Holy Land in the late nineteenth century and named some of the streets he was developing after the places he had visited: **Carmel Street**, **Cairo Street**, **Damascus Street**, **Jerusalem Street** and **Palestine Street**.

NUN STREET, NEWCASTLE UPON TYNE

Named after the Benedictine nuns of St Bartholomew's Priory, which stood on the site. Nearby **Strawberry Place** and **Strawberry Lane**, next to St James's Park football ground, recall the fields where the nuns grew strawberries.

ST GILES WAY AND ST GILES CRESCENT, WREXHAM

Named after the town's parish church with its glorious 136-foot-high Gothic tower, one of the Seven Wonders of Wales. Lying outside at the foot of the tower in a big stone tomb is Elihu Yale (1649-1721), benefactor of Yale University in Connecticut, USA. Boston-born Yale grew up near Wrexham in the family home Plas yn Ial, which means 'hall or house in a place called Ial'. The surname

Yale is an anglicisation of Ial. Thus Yale University is named after a Welsh valley.

ST JAMES'S CHURCHYARD, BRISTOL

A street of houses and shops that lay on the boundary of the churchyard of, er, St James's Church.

ST MARY AXE, LONDON

This street takes its name from the medieval church of St Mary Axe, which was demolished in the sixteenth century and replaced by a warehouse. The site is now occupied by a modern office block called Fitzwilliam House. The church was said to possess one of the three axes with which Atilla the Hun beheaded St Ursula and her 11,000 handmaidens after she refused to marry him. They met while she was passing through the Rhineland on her way back to Britain from a pilgrimage to Rome. Unsurprisingly, there is only one street called St Mary Axe in Britain.

SHANKILL ROAD, BELFAST

A road in west Belfast, the name Shankill is derived from the Irish *sean chille*, meaning 'old church', referring to the Church of St Patrick of the White Ford, which stood here beside a ford across the River Farset as far back as AD 455. The Farset gives its name to Belfast, which was founded on a sandy ford across the Farset - Béal Feirste, meaning 'at the mouth of the sandbar'.

WHITECHAPEL ROAD, LONDON

A good example of a street named after a specific church, Whitechapel Road takes its name from a thirteenth-century chapel with whitewashed stone walls that was built as a chapel of ease dedicated to St Mary, associated with the parish church of St Dunstan's in Stepney. In the seventeenth century, Stepney was divided into several new parishes and the chapel became the new parish church of the place named after its white walls, Whitechapel. The church was destroyed by bombing during the Blitz and just the footprint remains, surrounded by a small park, formerly St Mary's Park, but renamed in 1998 as Altab Ali Park in memory of a British Bangladeshi murdered nearby in 1978. The park also marks the place where **Whitechapel High Street** becomes Whitechapel Road.

The beginning part of the old Roman Road to Colchester, now the A11, Whitechapel Road starts at Aldgate as Whitechapel High Street and runs east for just over a mile where it becomes **Mile End Road**, named for the settlement a mile away from Aldgate.

PALACES AND MANSIONS

LEADENHALL STREET AND LEADENHALL MARKET, LONDON

These get their name from a fourteenth-century hall with a lead roof, belonging to the Neville family, that stood on the site until it was destroyed in the Great Fire of London in 1666.

ORMEAU ROAD, BELFAST

Laid out through south Belfast in the early nineteenth century, this road takes its name from a large Georgian house that the road ran past, Ormeau House, home of the Marquess of Donegall and the largest private house in Belfast. The name 'Ormeau' comes from the French word *orme*, meaning 'elm tree', suggesting that the grounds were noted for their elm trees. The house was demolished in the latter part of the nineteenth century and the grounds were opened as a municipal park in 1871 - the biggest and oldest public park in Belfast.

RED HOUSE LANE, BEXLEYHEATH, KENT

Named after Red House, completed in 1860 on a large plot of land in what was then the rural village of Upton. The house was designed by Philip Webb and William Morris as a family home for Morris and his new wife Jane, and is an early example of the Arts and Crafts style developed by Morris with the aim of reviving traditional craftsmanship and artisan skills. It is decorated with some of Morris's earliest wallpaper designs and murals by Edward Burne-Jones. It is now owned and run by the National Trust.

WHITEHALL, LONDON

Like Whitechapel Road on page 105, Whitehall was named for the white walls of a long-gone building, in this case Whitehall Palace. In 1512 the royal apartments at the Palace of Westminster were destroyed by fire and the king, Henry VIII, either had to squeeze in with the staff at Westminster while he was in London or stay downriver at Greenwich in the Palace of Placentia where he had been born in 1491. Proof that he chose the latter to begin with is that both his daughters were born at Greenwich, Mary in 1516 and Elizabeth in 1533.

The opportunity arose to build a new palace at Westminster in 1530 when the king's adviser, Cardinal Wolsey, fell from grace for failing to arrange the annulment of Henry's marriage to Katherine of Aragon. One of Wolsey's appointments was Archbishop of York, a position that entitled him to reside in York House, the archbishop's grand residence next to the Palace of Westminster. Henry helped himself to York Place and turned it into a vast, sprawling palace covering twenty-three acres, the largest palace in Europe. Wolsey had already spared no expense in turning York House into a palace fit for a Wolsey, and the walls were constructed of the finest white ashlar stone, hence the name Whitehall Palace. The name was doubly appropriate as White Hall was the term given to a building or great hall dedicated to festivities, something that Henry VIII excelled at. As William Shakespeare put it in *Henry VIII* (Act 4, Scene 1): 'Sir, / You must no more call it York-place, that's past; / For, since the cardinal fell, that title's lost; / 'Tis now the king's and call'd Whitehall.'

Whitehall Palace remained the principal palace of the Tudor and Stuart kings (and Oliver Cromwell as Lord Protector) until the reign of William III. In 1698 it burned down after one of Dutch William's Dutch servants, a washerwoman, set fire to a basket of linen she was attempting to dry by a charcoal fire and the conflagration spread through the ramshackle complex of old buildings. Only Inigo Jones's Banqueting House of 1622 survived, along with Henry VIII's wine cellar (now under the Ministry of Defence), **Queen Mary's Steps** - a set of stone steps and part of a riverside terrace built by Christopher Wren for Queen Mary II in 1691, now to be found against the east wall of the MOD - and, of course, the name Whitehall.

Today the street known as Whitehall is dominated by government buildings, including the Ministry of Defence, the Foreign Office and the Treasury, and the term Whitehall has come to refer to the bureaucratic institutions of government or the Civil Service in general, as exemplified by the slightly sinister aphorism attributed to the politician Douglas Jay - 'the gentleman in Whitehall knows best'.

Running off east at the north end of Whitehall is a small alleyway called **Craig's Court** that was laid out in 1690, when the palace was still standing, by Joseph Craig, described as a vestryman of St Martin's Church, now St Martin-in-the-Fields beside Trafalgar

Square. The alleyway opens out into a courtyard in front of the rather stately Harrington House, which was built after the fire in 1702 by William Stanhope, 1st Baron Harrington, who wanted a home close to court when Whitehall Palace was rebuilt. Alas, it never was and poor Baron Harrington found himself isolated miles away from the centre of power, which had moved to St James's Palace.

Remarkably, the little alleyway of Craig's Court played a significant role in the history of Britain's streets. In 1761 the Speaker of the House of Commons, Arthur Onslow (renowned for his integrity and the longest-serving Speaker ever, being in office for over thirty years), paid a visit to Harrington House but had to climb out through the roof of his carriage when it got stuck in the narrowest part of the alleyway, and was forced to walk in his fine shoes along the treacherous muddy track, as the streets in those days were unpaved. Badly shaken, Speaker Onslow oversaw on his return to Parliament the 1762 Westminster Paving Act legislating for the provision of raised pavements to enable pedestrians to walk above the grime and filth of the churned-up streets. Westminster thus set an example, followed soon afterwards, for the rest of Britain's streets.

A little further south off Whitehall is **Great Scotland Yard**, on the site of a house given to King Kenneth III of Scotland by King Edgar of England when he came to visit in 959. Subsequently Scottish royalty stayed at lodgings here when visiting London, the last royal to do so being Henry VIII's sister Margaret, widow of James IV of Scotland. Sir Robert Peel (see pages 77 and 126) opened the first Metropolitan Police Station here in 1829 and since the entrance to the station was in Great Scotland Yard, the street name became synonymous with the Metropolitan police, with every subsequent headquarters being named New Scotland Yard.

Horse Guards Avenue creates a grand approach to Horse Guards, which was built as the barracks and stables for the Household Cavalry and formed the main entrance to Whitehall Palace. When Whitehall Palace burned down, Horse Guards was rebuilt as the entrance to St James's Palace. Since St James's has remained as the monarch's senior official palace, the Horse Guards arch (through which only the monarch can ride) is still guarded by the Queen's Life Guard.

Richmond Terrace and **Richmond Terrace Mews**, now combined as Richmond House, stand on the site of the townhouse of Charles Stuart, 3rd Duke of Richmond and cousin of Charles II. The original Richmond House was built in 1660 just after the Restoration, on the former bowling green of Whitehall Palace. The facade of Richmond Terrace seen there today was built in 1822, while the Mews was built over in the 1980s to form government offices.

Derby Gate recalls the town residence of the Earls of Derby, which stood here in the sixteenth century, while **Canon Row** was where the canons of St Stephen's Royal Chapel in the Palace of Westminster had their lodgings.

Craven Passage and the adjoining **Craven Street** are named for the former landowners, the Craven family, later Earls of Craven, from Hampstead Marshall in Berkshire, who developed the area in the 1740s. The smart Georgian terraced houses of Craven Street have been home to some distinguished American residents, including Benjamin Franklin, who lived at No. 36 for sixteen years while acting as de facto ambassador for the American colonies before the American Revolutionary War; Vice President Aaron Burr, the man who killed Founding Father Alexander Hamilton in a duel; and Herman Melville, author of *Moby Dick*.

It was the Craven family, in the guise of William Craven, the 6th Baron Craven who, in 1780, built the cottage that gave their name to Craven Cottage, the home ground of London's oldest professional football club, Fulham FC. The cottage, which still stands in the corner of the football ground, occupies the site of a hunting lodge set in woods that belonged to Anne Boleyn.

CASTLES

CASTLE HILL, STIRLING

This runs up the hill on which Stirling Castle sits, while Edinburgh's **Castle Terrace** runs below the rock on which Edinburgh Castle is perched.

CASTLE STREET AND CASTLE PLACE, BELFAST

City-centre streets on the site of Belfast's Norman castle which, after a fairly bloody history and several rebuilds, was finally destroyed by a fire in 1708. A new Scots baronial-style Belfast Castle was built in a commanding position on **Cave Hill**, north of Belfast, in 1870 by the Marquess of Donegall. It was gifted to the city in 1934 and now serves as an events venue.

OTHER BUILDINGS

BAKEHOUSE LANE, DURHAM

This is the site of a long-lost bakehouse, while **Diamond Terrace** recalls the coal mined here - coal was known as 'black diamond' - along with **Pit Lane** and **Old Pit Terrace**.

BATH STREET, ABERYSTWYTH

Named after the public baths that opened on the street in 1880.

ORPHANAGE ROAD, ERDINGTON, BIRMINGHAM

Named after an orphanage built here in 1860 by pen manufacturer and philanthropist Josiah Mason.

BRIDGES AND CANALS

BRIGGATE, LEEDS

From the Old English *brycg*, meaning 'bridge', this street leads north into the city from Leeds Bridge across the River Aire. Intriguingly, Leeds Bridge, and hence Briggate, featured as the setting for the first-ever piece of moving film, showing traffic moving on the bridge, shot by Augustin Le Prince in October 1888.

GREAT BRIDGEWATER STREET, MANCHESTER

Named after the Bridgewater Canal, the world's first modern canal, which ended here. It was built by the Earl of Bridgewater in 1761 to transport coal from his mines at Worsley to the centre of Manchester. **Canal Street** runs alongside the Rochdale Canal, while **Quay Street** was laid out in the eighteenth century to provide access from the city centre to Edward Byrom's quay on the River Irwell. Britain's first purpose-built television studios, Granada Studios, where the Beatles gave their first-ever television performance, stand on Quay Street.

WELLS AND CONDUITS

CHALYBEATE STREET, ABERYSTWYTH

Named after a chalybeate well, fed by spring water containing iron salts, discovered here at the end of the eighteenth century.

GOSWELL ROAD, CLERKENWELL, LONDON

The name comes from 'God's Well', one of the many wells in the Clerkenwell area springing up from the River Fleet. **Clerkenwell Road**, which runs west off Goswell Road, was named after the Clerks' Well, while nearby **Skinner Street** recalls the Skinners' Well. Sadler's Wells theatre on Rosebery Avenue was built in 1683 by Thomas Sadler beside a well called Islington Spa, which it was claimed possessed medicinal properties similar to those of the waters at Tunbridge Wells in Kent.

WELL LANE, LINCOLN

Running off Lincoln's oldest street, Steep Hill, this lane, marked by a Victorian cast-iron well pump, recalls the natural springs that emerged from the escarpment on which Lincoln Cathedral stands and provided an important source of water for Lincoln.

WELLS ROAD, WELL WAY AND SPA DRIVE, EPSOM, SURREY

Marking the springs that provided water rich in magnesium sulphate, from which came the medicinal Epsom salts that made Epsom famous as a spa town in the eighteenth century. The springs led indirectly to Britain's richest horse race, the Epsom Derby, first run on the Epsom Downs in 1780. The Earl of Derby, after whom it is named, had a house in nearby Carshalton, where he would stay while taking the cure at Epsom, as did many of his friends, and it was at a party in one of those houses, the Oaks, that they came up with the idea for the race.

WHITE CONDUIT STREET, ISLINGTON, LONDON

Just west of Islington High Street stood a conduit known as the White Conduit after the small, white-walled building that covered the cistern, and this is what gave the street its name. The conduit had been set up in the fifteenth century to pipe water to the Charterhouse Priory next to Smithfield Market, but it slowly fell out of use and the land around it was laid out as a public open space called White Conduit Fields. At the time that Pentonville was being developed, White Conduit Fields became a venue for cricket and in 1782 the exclusive White Conduit Cricket Club was formed from a mix of hired professionals and aristocratic amateurs such as Charles Lennox, 4th Duke of Richmond, and the Earl of Winchilsea, patrons of the Star and Garter tavern on Pall Mall, where the rules of cricket were drawn up. They eventually decided that White Conduit Fields was too public and instructed one of the hired men, Yorkshire bowler Thomas Lord, to find them a piece of private land where they could play. He obtained a lease on some land west along the New Road in Marylebone (see page 103), the forerunner to Lords Cricket Ground, and the White Conduit Club morphed into the Marylebone Cricket Club, or MCC.

WINDMILLS

MILL ROAD, CAMBRIDGE

Once a quiet lane leading south-east out of Cambridge, the street was named after a windmill that stood here. It is now famous for the Mill Road Winter Fair. Writers Douglas Adams (*The Hitch Hiker's Guide to the Galaxy*), Fred Hoyle (*A for Andromeda*), Ronald Searle (*St Trinian's*) and Tom Sharpe (*Wilt*) have all lived on Mill Road.

WINDMILL CROFT, GLASGOW

Recalls a windmill built here by landowner Sir George Elphinstone in the sixteenth century for the use of his tenants. The windmill was demolished in 1749.

CROSSES AND CROSSROADS

CHARING CROSS ROAD, LONDON

Charing Cross Road leads north from Charing Cross, the junction being named after a cross standing in what was the small village of Charing. This was the last of the twelve crosses that Edward I had erected to mark each of the twelve places where the funeral cortège of his wife Eleanor rested during the journey from Harby in Nottinghamshire, where she died in 1290, to Westminster Abbey. Charing comes from the Old English *cierran*, meaning 'to curve' or 'to bend', reflecting how the village of Charing stood beside a curve or bend in the River Thames.

Charing Cross Road was renowned for its bookshops and in 1987 the street gained worldwide fame when the film *84 Charing Cross Road* was released, starring Anne Bancroft and Anthony Hopkins. The film was based on a book by Helene Hanff that charts the correspondence she had in 1945 with a bookshop called Marks & Co., which stood at No. 84 Charing Cross Road.

In the *Harry Potter* stories, the Leaky Cauldron stands on Charing Cross Road, a favourite with author J. K. Rowling, who made Charing Cross Road the location for the office of her fictional private detective, Cormoran Strike.

KING'S CROSS ROAD, LONDON

King's Cross Road takes its name from the district in which it stands, as does King's Cross Station, the biggest station in the world when it was opened in 1851 for crowds coming into London to attend the Great Exhibition in Hyde Park, and the terminus for Harry Potter's Hogwarts Express. King's Cross was formerly a village called Battle

Bridge, a corruption of the Broad Ford Bridge which crossed the River Fleet here. It takes its current name from a major crossroads on which a huge, two-storey octagonal monument to George IV, sixty feet high with an eleven-foot-high statue of the king on top, was erected in 1830. The first floor was occupied by a camera obscura while the ground floor served first as a police station and then a pub. The monument was much mocked and came down in 1845, but the name King's Cross stuck, making King's Cross Road a good example of a street named after a crossroads (as opposed to an actual cross, like Charing Cross Road).

Another name for a crossroads is 'carfax', from the Latin word *quadrifurcus*, meaning 'four-pronged' or 'four-forked', via the French word *carrefour*. The ancient crossroads at the centre of Oxford where the four streets from the old city gates meet is named **Carfax**, as is the central area in the old market town of Horsham in Sussex.

BATTLES,
WAR HEROES
AND POLITICAL
FIGURES

Streets named after national heroes, politicians and events such as battles that were thought to be worth honouring can give a useful insight into our history.

BATTLE OF TRAFALGAR

By far the most common name in this category celebrates Admiral Lord Nelson, victor of the Battle of Trafalgar in 1805. Virtually every city has a **Nelson Street** or a **Nelson Road** - there are some three hundred of them - and if you add in all the Walks and Avenues and Squares and Drives, there are over five hundred streets that commemorate him.

COLLINGWOOD STREET, NEWCASTLE UPON TYNE
Named for Admiral Lord Collingwood, born in Newcastle in 1750, who was Nelson's second-in-command at the Battle of Trafalgar, at which his ship the *Royal Sovereign* fired the opening shots. When Nelson fell, Collingwood took command and saw the fleet through to victory without the loss of a single ship.

NELSON STREET, BRISTOL
Formerly Grape Lane, a variant of Grope Lane (see page 198), this street was renamed in honour of the victor of the Battle of Trafalgar. Thank goodness.

TRAFALGAR SQUARE, LONDON
London's ceremonial square was laid out over eighteen years between 1826 and 1844 on the site of the old Royal Mews and named in celebration of Admiral Nelson's victory over the French at the Battle of Trafalgar. Nelson himself stands at the top of a 184-foot column at the south end of the square, gazing south-west towards

the fleet at Portsmouth. Adolf Hitler planned to have Nelson's Column dismantled and resurrected in Berlin as a symbol of his expected subjugation of Britain. The square now serves as a gathering place for rallies, riots, national sporting celebrations, concerts and New Year's Eve revelries.

OTHER BATTLES

AGINCOURT ROAD, COVENTRY AND PORTSMOUTH

Named for Henry V's celebrated victory over the French at the Battle of Agincourt in 1415. It was at this battle that the famous 'V' sign was first used, with the English and Welsh archers sticking up two fingers to the French to show that they still had their firing fingers, which would have been cut off had they been captured. There are ten Agincourt Roads in Britain and some twenty Agincourt Streets, Drives and Squares altogether. Belfast has an **Agincourt Street** and an **Agincourt Avenue**.

BULLER ROAD, THORNTON HEATH, LONDON

Named after General Redvers Buller, VC, commander-in-chief of the British forces in South Africa during the early months of the Second Boer War (1899-1902), this is one of several streets of an Edwardian housing development named after figures involved in the Boer War, a recent event when the development was built.

Hamilton Road is named after Sir Ian Hamilton, in charge of the British troops at the Siege of Ladysmith (1899-1900). **Hunter Road** is named after General Sir Archibald Hunter, commander at the Siege of Ladysmith and the capture of Pretoria. **Kitchener Road** is named after Earl Kitchener, commander-in-chief of the British forces in South Africa during the later months of the war, who later found fame as the face of the famous First World War recruiting poster by Albert Leete, 'Lord Kitchener Wants You'. **Milner Road** is named after Alfred Milner, Governor of the Cape Colony and High Commissioner for Southern Africa from 1897 to 1901.

The Boer War was fresh in the memory when many Edwardian housing developments were being built and there are many streets named after the figures and battles associated with the war. Tottenham has a Buller Road and a **Redvers Road** as well as a **Mafeking Road**, named in memory of the 217-day Siege of Mafeking in 1899-1901. There is a Mafeking Road in Brighton as well as a **Ladysmith Road** and **Kimberley Road**, all named after famous sieges during the Boer War, as well as a Redvers Road and a Buller Road. Chesterfield in Derbyshire has a **Redvers Buller Road**, adjacent to **Lord Roberts Road**, named after another commander of British forces during the Boer War, and a **Baden Powell Road**, named after the commander of the British garrison during the Siege of Mafeking.

GREAT MARLBOROUGH STREET, LONDON

This street was constructed just after John Churchill, 1st Duke of Marlborough, had led the English to victory against the French at the Battle of Blenheim in 1704 during the War of the Spanish Succession (1701-14), and was named after him in celebration.

PORTOBELLO ROAD, LONDON

Home to the world's largest antiques market, attracting visitors from all over the globe. Originally Porto Bello Lane, it takes its name from Porto Bello Farm, which was built in 1740 and was named after a famous victory in 1739, when the Royal Navy under Admiral Vernon captured the port of Portobelo in Central America from the Spanish during the War of Jenkins' Ear (1739-48). This was the occasion that

'Rule Britannia' was written to celebrate and many places were named in its honour, including the suburb of Portobello in Edinburgh. Porto Bello Lane, which ran through farmland, was eventually renamed Portobello Road when the area became developed during the second half of the nineteenth century. Admiral Vernon is remembered by **Vernon Yard**, which runs off Portobello Road. The road found further fame in the 1999 film *Notting Hill* as the location for the Travel Book Company run by the lead character William Thacker, played by Hugh Grant.

RODNEY STREET, PENTONVILLE, LONDON

Named after Admiral Rodney, best known for defeating the French navy at the Battle of the Saintes in the Caribbean in 1782 during the American Revolutionary War (1775-83). Henry Penton, after whom Pentonville is named (see page 162), had just stepped down as Lord of the Admiralty at the time and was a great admirer of Rodney.

WATERLOO ROAD AND WATERLOO BRIDGE, LONDON

Named, in addition to Waterloo Station, in honour of the Duke of Wellington's victory over the French at the Battle of Waterloo in 1815. There are something like one hundred and forty-five Waterloo Roads in Britain, and two hundred Wellington Roads as well as fifty Wellesley Roads, so called after the duke's family name.

Nottingham has a Waterloo Road, for instance, among a number of streets in the city recalling various battles. **Lucknow Avenue** recalls the Siege of Lucknow during the Indian Rebellion of 1857. **Nile Street** celebrates the Battle of the Nile of 1798, when Lord Nelson defeated a French fleet near the Nile Delta in Egypt. Nearby are **Trafalgar Street** and **Nelson Street**, while **Isandula Road** and **Zulu Road** recall the Battle of Isandlwana during the Anglo-Zulu War of 1879.

FIRST AND SECOND WORLD WARS

ARNHEM ROAD, WOLVERHAMPTON

One of a cluster of streets named for Second World War battles
that local men took part in. Others include **Tobruk Walk**
and **Alamein Road**.

BERNARD CASSIDY STREET, CANNING TOWN, LONDON

Named after Lieutenant Bernard Cassidy, VC, of the Lancashire
Fusiliers, who was born in Canning Town. He was awarded the
Victoria Cross posthumously for his actions in holding the line at
Fampoux during the Battle of Arras in April 1917, when his men were
surrounded. Cassidy was killed and his body was never recovered. He
was twenty-five years old.

CAMBRAI AVENUE, CHICHESTER

Remembering the Battle of Cambrai of 1917.

JACK CORNWELL STREET, MANOR PARK, LONDON

Born a few miles away in Leyton, 'Jutland' Jack Cornwell joined the
Royal Navy in 1915 at the age of fifteen and served on the cruiser HMS
Chester. When she came under fire at the Battle of Jutland in May
1916, Cornwell was mortally wounded but remained at his post when
the rest of the gun crew were killed. He died of his wounds two days
later and was posthumously awarded the Victoria Cross, becoming
the third-youngest recipient.

JAMES TOWERS WAY, PRESTON

Born in Broughton, a suburb of Preston, in 1897, James Towers joined
the British army in 1915 while still under age. He received his Victoria

Cross for volunteering to find and rescue a company of men trapped by the Germans in the village of Mericourt and leading them to safety during the Hundred Days Offensive in 1918.

MONS AVENUE, ROCHDALE

One of a cluster of five streets near the Rochdale football stadium named after battles of the Great War, including **Marne Crescent**, **Verdun Crescent** and two streets named after naval battles, **Jutland Avenue** and **Falkland Avenue**.

POLITICIANS AND REFORMERS

ELIZABETH FRY ROAD, NORWICH

Named in honour of Elizabeth Fry (1780-1845), one of Norwich's most famous daughters, who campaigned tirelessly for prison reform and whose image graced the reverse side of the old paper £5 note until it was replaced by the new polymer note in 2016.

GREY STREET, NEWCASTLE UPON TYNE

Sir John Betjeman once said of Grey Street, 'As for the curve of Grey Street . . . not even Regent Street, even old Regent Street London, can compare with that descending subtle curve.' Newcastle's most famous thoroughfare, Grey Street is often described as one of the finest streets in England and leads from the River Tyne up to Grey's Monument, in memory, like Grey Street itself, of prime minister Charles Grey, the 2nd Earl Grey (1764-1845), after whom Earl Grey tea is named. As prime minister, he advocated Catholic emancipation and enacted both the Abolition of Slavery Act of 1833, abolishing slavery throughout the British Empire, and the Great Reform Act of 1832, greatly expanding the franchise to all male property owners and professionals regardless of income. The Act itself is remembered by a number of street names, including **Reform Street** in Dundee and Hull and **Reform Road** in Maidenhead, Berkshire.

HUSKISSON STREET, LIVERPOOL

This smart street running east from Liverpool Cathedral commemorates the Liverpool MP William Huskisson, who became the first person ever to be killed in a railway accident when he was knocked down by Stephenson's Rocket during the opening of the Liverpool and Manchester Railway on 15 September 1830.

LIVERPOOL STREET, LONDON

Named after Lord Liverpool, prime minister from 1812, following the assassination of Spencer Perceval, to 1827.

Liverpool (the place, not the person) has a clutch of streets named after nineteenth-century prime ministers. **Canning Street** is named for George Canning, MP for Liverpool between 1812 and 1823. He served as prime minister for just 118 days, the shortest-ever term as prime minister, and died in office. **Gladstone Road**, **Street** and **Avenue** are named in honour of the 'Grand Old Man' William Gladstone, four times prime minister, who was born in Liverpool at 62 Rodney Street (see page 122), in 1809 and left office at the age of eighty-four, the oldest person ever to serve as prime minister and the only one to serve four terms. **Beaconsfield Street** is named after Benjamin Disraeli, Lord Beaconsfield, who served twice as prime minister, succeeded on each occasion by Gladstone. **Salisbury Road** is named for Robert Gascoyne-Cecil, 3rd Marquess of Salisbury, three times prime minister and descendant of Elizabeth I's senior councillor Lord Burghley. He established the colony of Rhodesia (now Zimbabwe) in southern Africa and the capital was named Salisbury after him. It is now Harare. He retired in 1902 after leading the government through the Boer War and was succeeded by his nephew Arthur Balfour. 'Bob's your uncle', you might say.

NELSON MANDELA PLACE, GLASGOW

Home of the South African consulate, this street, originally St George's Place, was renamed in recognition of the anti-apartheid campaigner Nelson Mandela in 1986, as a powerful political statement at the height of the struggles to end apartheid in South Africa. Also **Mandela Way** in south London, a newly built street running adjacent to the Old Kent Road, which was named after Mandela had become the first black President of South Africa to be elected, and **Nelson Mandela Road** in Blackheath in south-east London.

OPIE STREET, NORWICH

Named for poet, Romantic novelist and philanthropist Amelia Opie, born in Norwich in 1769. She campaigned for women's education and the abolition of slavery - hers was the first of the 187,000 women's names on a petition presented to Parliament to abolish slavery by the Ladies Anti-Slavery Society (founded by her). She is one of the few women included in the commemorative painting by Benjamin Robert Haydon of the World Anti-Slavery Convention held in London in 1840.

PEEL STREET, GLASGOW

Named after Sir Robert Peel (1788-1850) who, as home secretary, founded the Metropolitan Police Service in 1829, since which time policemen have variously been known as 'peelers' and 'bobbies' after him (see also page 77). He was twice prime minister and a founder of the Conservative Party but was brought down after forcing through the Repeal of the Corn Laws in 1846, which reduced the price of food for ordinary Britons. A supporter of the Protestant Orange cause in Ireland, he was often greeted by opponents as 'Orange Peel'.

PITT STREET, NEWCASTLE UPON TYNE

There are forty-five Pitt Streets in Britain, named for William Pitt the Younger (1759-1806), who, at the age of twenty-four, became the youngest-ever prime minister of Britain. He is remembered for guiding Britain safely through the French Revolution and the early stages of the Napoleonic Wars, and also for engineering the Acts of Union with Ireland in 1800. The Union itself is recalled by **Union Street** in Aberdeen, laid out at the beginning of the nineteenth century to relieve the cramped streets of the old centre of the city. Union Street crosses the valley of the River Denburn via the 130-foot-long **Union Bridge**, the largest single-span granite bridge in the world. Aberdeen also has a **Union Row** and a **Union Terrace**.

WINSTON CHURCHILL AVENUE, PORTSMOUTH

Named in honour of Britain's wartime prime minster, this is the only Winston Churchill Avenue in Britain. There are over a hundred Churchill Roads and numerous Churchill Avenues and Streets.

10

ROYAL CONNECTIONS

It was the Georgians who began naming their streets after particular kings and queens. Before then there were plenty of non-specific King's Ways and Queen's Ways, but the proliferation of new streets being laid out with Teutonic efficiency during the eighteenth century provided ample opportunity to honour the new Hanoverian kings. There have been lots of Georges - six, to be precise - so it is hardly surprising there are lots of George Streets, but even though there was only one queen by her name, the most common royal street name is **Victoria Road**. She did reign for over sixty years and the number of streets multiplied exponentially under the Victorians, so, again, perhaps that is not so surprising. Also among the top forty is **Albert Road**, named for Queen Victoria's consort Prince Albert. As well as sharing a museum, the V&A, Victoria and Albert each have an embankment in London - the **Victoria Embankment**, running north of the Thames, and the **Albert Embankment** running south of the Thames - both constructed during Queen Victoria's reign.

Victoria Road, Kensington, was named as the UK's most expensive street in 2015. Residents have included the King of Malaysia, actor Dustin Hoffman, poet Henry Newbolt ('Play up! Play up! And play the game!') and ballet dancer Rudolf Nureyev. Victoria Road, Formby, is known as Merseyside's Millionaire's Row. Liverpool manager Jürgen Klopp lives there and residents have included Leicester manager Brendan Rodgers and footballers Steven Gerrard, Duncan Ferguson, Wayne Rooney and Alan Shearer.

KINGS

Other royals do get a look-in, however. There are streets named after kings Alfred, Arthur, Charles, Edward, George, Henry, James, John and William. Some of them even have their very own street.

Edward VII has his own **King Edward VII Avenue** in Windsor, and George IV has his own **George IV Bridge** in Edinburgh, which links the Royal Mile (see page 134) in the Old Town to Princes Street in the New Town and on which construction began during his reign in 1827. George V has quite a few streets named **George V Avenue**, **Drive** or **Road** after him, while for George VI there are six streets called **King George VI Avenue** (and one **Drive** in Hove in Sussex).

Portsmouth gives Henry I his own **King Henry I Street,** for no apparent reason, and Richard I has **King Richard I Street** in honour of the fact that he gave Portsmouth its first charter in 1194. Richard also gets the slightly less respectful **King Dick's Lane** in Bristol, which was an ancient right of way through the Kingswood Forest during his reign. Henry V, meanwhile, has **King Henry V Drive** in Monmouth, where he was born in 1386.

The Wessex town of Chard in Somerset has a number of streets dedicated to the local kings of Wessex: **King Athelstan Drive, King Ceol Close, King Cerdic Close, King Cuthred Close** and **King Ine Close**. Colchester in Essex has a **King Coel Road** based on the local legend that says the town's name comes from 'Coel-caster', or fortress of Coel. Coel was a fourth-century Celtic king said to be the father of St Helena, mother of the Roman emperor Constantine the Great, and also the subject of the nursery rhyme 'Old King Cole'. Alas, Colchester was actually named for the River Colne, as in 'Colne-chester', fortress on the River Colne.

Situated on top of Dover's Shakespeare Cliff is **King Lear's Way**, reflecting the fact that Dover is mentioned eleven times in Shakespeare's eponymous play, and is indeed where King Lear dies at the end of the play. King Offa of Mercia granted another coastal location, Bexhill in Sussex, its first charter in AD 771 and is rewarded with **King Offa Way**.

QUEENS

As for queens, Adelaide (consort of William IV), Alexandra (consort of Edward VII), Anne, Charlotte (consort of George III), Eleanor of Castile and Eleanor of Aquitaine (consorts of Edward I and Henry II respectively), Elizabeth I and II, Margaret (usually of Anjou, consort of Henry VI), Mary and, of course, Victoria each have numerous streets named in their honour.

Queen Elizabeth II has her own **Queen Elizabeth II Bridge** over the River Thames at Dartford. Also in Kent, Ramsgate has a **Queen Bertha Road** and Margate a **Queen Bertha's Avenue**, each named for the Saxon Queen Bertha of Kent who persuaded her husband King Ethelbert to convert to Christianity under St Augustine in AD 597.

Katherine Parr, sixth wife of Henry VIII, has **Queen Katherine Street** and **Queen Katherines Avenue** in Kendal in the Lake District, where she was born in 1512.

Queen Isabella Way in the City of London commemorates Edward II's consort Queen Isabella, who is thought to have had her husband murdered at Berkeley Castle so that she could put her young son Edward III on the throne and rule through him as regent with her lover, Roger Mortimer. The street runs beside the ruined Christ Church Greyfriars where she was buried in 1358.

Queen Square, Bristol, is named in honour of Queen Anne, after she visited Bristol in 1702. Woodes Rogers, captain of the ship that rescued Alexander Selkirk from Juan Fernandez Island in the South Pacific in 1709 (the inspiration for *Robinson Crusoe*), lived in the square, which is just round the corner from the ancient Llandoger Trow pub where author Daniel Defoe is said to have met Alexander

Selkirk and heard his story. A plaque in the square states that the first US consulate was established in Queen Square in 1792, which seems apposite since America may well have been named after the Bristol merchant Richard Amerike who sponsored John Cabot's voyage of discovery to the New World in 1497. Unfortunately the plaque is wrong: the first-ever US consulate was established two years earlier in Liverpool by James Maury.

Covering all the bases are **King and Queen Street** in Walworth and **King and Queen Close** in Eltham, both in south-east London.

OTHER ROYAL ASSOCIATIONS

BELFAST

* **Prince Edward Drive** in Belfast dates from the 1930s and is one of the few street names to honour the prince who became Edward VIII and then abdicated.

BIRMINGHAM

* **Queensway**. Named in honour of Queen Elizabeth II, who opened it in 1971. The story goes that the name Queensway was originally meant to refer just to one of the tunnels on the ring road, with the rest of the road being called The Ringway, but after the Queen announced, 'I name this road the Queensway,' no one had the courage to demur and so Queensway became the name for the whole ring road.

BRIGHTON

* **Pavilion Parade**. This street runs along the front of the Royal Pavilion, begun in 1787 as a seaside retreat for the Prince Regent,

later George IV. Nearby **Princes Street**, **George Street** and **William Street** are all named for Prince George and his brother William IV, who both enjoyed their stays at the Pavilion. The presence of royalty encouraged the rapid expansion of Brighton and the many royal street names reflect this, such as **Regent Square**, **Regent Street** and **Queen Square**.

CARDIFF

* **King Edward VII Avenue**. Avenue that runs through the middle of Cardiff's Civic Centre, much of which was constructed during the reign of Edward VII. **Queen Street**, Cardiff's main shopping thoroughfare, was renamed in honour of Queen Victoria in 1886. **Plantagenet Street** and **Tudor Street** commemorate the royal houses that met at Bosworth Field in 1485 when Henry VII, first of the Welsh Tudors, defeated Richard III, last of the Angevin Plantagenets.

EDINBURGH

* **George Street**, the central street of Edinburgh's New Town, the world's most complete Georgian townscape, is so called in honour of George III, for it was laid out in the 1760s and 1770s during his reign. George Street runs between the New Town's two main squares, **St Andrew Square**, named for the patron saint of Scotland, and **Charlotte Square**, named in honour of George III's consort Queen Charlotte, who put up Britain's first Christmas tree at Windsor in 1800.

* **Princes Street**. Three-quarters of a mile in length and running dead straight from east to west, Princes Street marks the boundary between Edinburgh's Old Town and New Town and is the city's main shopping street. Originally a country lane called Lang Dykes ('long ditch'), it was the first part of the New Town to be developed in 1770 and was going to be called St Giles Street after Edinburgh's patron saint, but George III objected, apparently because he associated the name with the St Giles slum in London. Instead it was named Prince's Street in honour of the Prince of Wales, the future George IV. At some point the apostrophe was dropped in favour of the current version of the name, Princes Street.

The street is punctuated at each end by two huge Victorian railway hotels, the Balmoral, originally the North British Railway Station Hotel, at the eastern end, and the Waldorf Astoria Caledonian Hotel at the western end, built by the Caledonian Railway above the former Princes Street Station. The most notable landmark on Princes Street is the Victorian-Gothic Scott Monument, in honour of Sir Walter Scott (1771-1832). At just over two hundred feet high, it is the second-largest monument to an author in the world, the largest being that to the Cuban freedom writer José Martí (1853-95), in Havana, which is a whopping 358 feet high.

* **The Royal Mile**, located in Edinburgh's Old Town, is the 'largest, longest and finest street in the world', according to Daniel Defoe, and is so called because it runs between two of Scotland's pre-eminent historic royal sites. It leads downhill from Edinburgh Castle - where Mary, Queen of Scots, gave birth to the first British monarch, the future James VI of Scotland and James I of England in 1566 - to the Palace of Holyroodhouse, today the British monarch's official residence in Scotland. It was first referred to as the Royal Mile in 1901, in W. M. Gilbert's *Edinburgh in the Nineteenth Century*, in which he writes of the 'castle and palace and the royal mile between'. Actually one mile and 107 yards long, or what the people of Edinburgh call 'a Scots mile', the Royal Mile is made up of a number of different streets: **Castlehill**, the hill leading up to the castle; **Lawnmarket**, derived from the old linen

market; **High Street**; **Canongate**, the route taken into town by the Augustinian canons of Holyrood Abbey; and the short stretch of **Abbey Strand**, marking the boundary of the old abbey precincts. Until 1880, fugitives were able to take sanctuary in the Abbey Strand, as recalled by the name of the Abbey Sanctuary gift shop housed in a fine sixteenth-century gabled terrace at the gates of the palace. Brass studs spelling out an 'S' for sanctuary are set in the road.

The Royal Mile is the main street of Edinburgh's Old Town, and indeed of Scotland's capital and hence Scotland itself. About a third of the way down from the castle is **Parliament Square**, named for Parliament House, home of the Scottish parliament from 1639 until the Union of England and Scotland in 1707 - and now home to Scotland's Supreme Court. In the middle of the square is St Giles' Cathedral, senior church of the Scottish Presbyterians and built in 1495 on the site of Edinburgh's first church. Outside the west door is the Heart of Midlothian, a heart-shaped set of stones in the pavement marking the site of the Old Tolbooth from where Edinburgh was administered before 1617. This is where Hearts football club gets its name. Scotland's first lead statue - depicting Charles II as a Roman emperor atop a horse - stands outside Parliament House.

In East Parliament Square stands a statue of James Braidwood (1800-1861), 'Father of the British Fire Service' and founder of the world's first municipal fire service in Edinburgh in 1824. A cabinet maker by trade, he went on to become the first director of what became the London Fire Brigade and died fighting the infamous Tooley Street Fire that raged for two weeks at Cotton Wharf in London in 1861.

At the bottom of the Royal Mile, where Canongate meets Abbey Strand, is the new Scottish Parliament Building, opened in 2004.

GLASGOW

* **George Square**. Named after George III, who was on the throne when Glasgow's central square opened in 1787. It was originally a private square for the surrounding houses, but after the local people constantly broke down the railings, the authorities made it a public square and it has been Glasgow's main square and meeting place ever since.

* **Queen Mary Terrace**. Langside, where Queen Mary Terrace is located, keeps alive the memory of Mary, Queen of Scots, whose forces faced their final defeat at the Battle of Langside in 1568. **Hamilton Avenue** recalls the commander of Mary's army, Lord Claud Hamilton; her secretary Maitland of Lethington is remembered by **Maitland Avenue** and **Lethington Avenue**; while **Beaton Road**, **Seyton Avenue** and **Carmichael Road** commemorate her ladies-in-waiting, the four Marys, as celebrated in the old ballad - 'There was Mary Beaton, and Mary Seyton / And Mary Carmichael and me [Mary Fleming]' (although the third Mary was actually Mary Livingston, not Mary Carmichael). **Queen Mary Street** in east Glasgow near Celtic Park runs by the site of Barrowfield House, one of many houses where Queen Mary was said to have slept the night.

LIVERPOOL

* **Jubilee Drive**. Kensington in Liverpool, an area of Victorian terraces, often has clusters of related names, and running off Jubilee Drive, celebrating Queen Victoria's Golden Jubilee in 1887, are: **Albert Edward Road**, named for the Prince of Wales, the future Edward VII; **Empress Road**, named after Queen Victoria,

Empress of India; **Leopold Road**, named after Queen Victoria and Prince Albert's mutual uncle Leopold I of Belgium; and **Albany Road** and **Connaught Road**, named after the titles of two of the sons of Victoria and Albert. Nearby is **Brunswick Road**, honouring Caroline of Brunswick, wife of George IV.

LONDON

* **Black Prince Road**, in Lambeth, is named after Edward III's eldest son, Edward, Prince of Wales, father of Richard II, who was named for his black shield with three white ostrich feathers. He was the first Prince of Wales to adopt the three ostrich feathers on his badge and the story goes that he took the crest from the body of King John of Bohemia, who was killed at the Battle of Crécy in 1346. He was given the title Duke of Cornwall, becoming the first English duke in 1337, and owned land in Lambeth, hence the name of the street and the reason why the Duchy of Cornwall still owns a lot of land in this part of south London.

* **Cromwell Road**. Although Lord Protector Oliver Cromwell was not strictly royal, he was offered the crown but turned it down. Cromwell Road was part of the redevelopment of the whole area for the Great Exhibition of 1851, as recalled by **Exhibition Road**. Prince Albert himself apparently chose to name the street after Cromwell House, which stood near Hyde Park and was where the Lord Protector lived when in London. The house itself was, of course, named after Oliver Cromwell.

* **Denmark Street**. This short street off Charing Cross Road at St Giles Circus was named in honour of Prince George of Denmark, consort of Queen Anne. In the 1960s it became known as **Tin Pan Alley**, because it was home to numerous music publishers and songwriters. The music journals *Melody Maker* and the

New Musical Express were founded here, and in the 1960s and 1970s artists such as the Kinks, Jimmy Page, David Bowie, the Rolling Stones and Jimi Hendrix all recorded songs at the various recording studios on Denmark Street - when not socialising at La Gioconda café at No. 9. In 1970 Bernie Taupin and Elton John wrote Elton's first No. 1 hit, 'Your Song', at No. 20. The name Tin Pan Alley comes from New York in America: in the first half of the twentieth century, New York's music publishing businesses were concentrated on narrow West 28th Street, just off Broadway. Songwriters from all over America would come to West 28th Street to demonstrate their songs and, according to an article by Monroe Rosenfield, composer of 'Johnny Get Your Gun', in the *New York Herald*, the sound of umpteen different tunes being bashed out on tinny pianos in all the different offices was like the banging of tin pans in an alleyway. And so Tin Pan Alley came to refer to the music business in general.

* **King William Street**, in the City of London, is named for William IV, who was on the throne when the street was being laid out between 1829 and 1835.

* **Little Britain**. The street in Smithfield where the *Spectator* magazine was first printed in 1711 was named after the Dukes of Brittany, sovereigns of the Duchy of Brittany, who had a house there.

* **Pall Mall**. 'So I went into St. James's Park, where I saw the Duke of York playing at Pelemele, the first time that ever I saw the sport.' Thus reads the entry to Samuel Pepys's diary for 2 April 1661. Pelemele is a game not unlike croquet that originated in Italy as *pallamaglio*, a combination of *palla* (ball) and *maglio* (mallet), and was explained in a journal of 1621: 'A paille mall is a wooden

hammer set to the end of a long staff to strike a boule with, at which game noblemen and gentlemen in France doe play much.' Mary, Queen of Scots, who had spent her childhood in France while being lined up to marry the dauphin, introduced the game into Scotland and to her son James VI of Scotland, who brought it down to London when he became James I of England.

An unpaved alleyway running east to west between two rows of elm trees and leading through fields to the back of St James's Palace was found to be perfect for playing pall-mall. Eventually, though, the alleyway became used as a rat run for carriages and the players were blinded by the clouds of dust thrown up by their wheels. When Charles II was restored to the throne, he had a royal pall-mall alley laid out to the south on the main approach road to St James's Palace, which ran parallel with the original alleyway. With the old main road now blocked, the original pall-mall alley was paved and upgraded in 1661 into a street to replace it. The new street was at first named Catherine Street in honour of Charles II's wife Catherine of Braganza, but since everyone referred to it as the old pall-mall alley, Pall Mall was the name for the street that stuck.

* The new royal pall-mall alley to the south eventually became **The Mall**, named, not as in many other places because it was a promenade, but because of its association with pall-mall. In fact, the craze for pall-mall eventually died out with the Stuarts, and The Mall, on the edge of St James's Park and free of traffic, did become a fashionable promenade. In 1903 it was widened to become a wide processional avenue in honour of Queen Victoria, linking Admiralty Arch with the vast Queen Victoria memorial in front of Buckingham Palace. The site of the actual pall-mall alley survives alongside The Mall and is now known as the **Horse Ride**.

* In between the Mall and Pall Mall is **Carlton House Terrace**, built by John Nash in 1830 on the site of Carlton House, the home of Henry Boyle, Baron Carleton (Carleton being a village in Yorkshire where the Boyle family had land). Boyle was also MP for Cambridge, where you can find **Carlton Way** and the Carlton Arms pub both named after him.

Carlton House, or Carleton House - somewhere along the line the 'e' got dropped - was one of many large houses built along the newly developed Pall Mall which, because of its proximity to St James's Palace, became a fashionable place to live. One example is Marlborough House, designed by Sir Christopher Wren in 1711 for Queen Anne's confidante, Sarah, the Duchess of Marlborough, and accessed along **Marlborough Road**. Also **Cleveland Row**, named for Charles II's favourite mistress Barbara Villiers, Duchess of Cleveland, who lived there in Cleveland House, now Bridgewater House, conveniently close to the palace.

* **St James's Street**, **St James's Square**, **St James's Place** and the whole area of St James's takes its name from St James's Palace, which was built by Henry VIII and was the principal royal palace until Queen Victoria moved into Buckingham Palace - foreign ambassadors are still accredited to the Court of St James's, hence **Ambassadors' Court**. St James's Palace was built on the site of St James's Hospital, a leper hospital founded by the people of London before the Norman Conquest. Hospitals were often dedicated to St James the Less, one of the Twelve Apostles, first Bishop of Jerusalem and possibly the brother or cousin of Jesus, since he was considered so honourable that simply touching his garments was enough to heal someone.

* The grassland behind St James's Palace, known as St James's Fields, was developed in the late seventeenth century by one of Charles II's courtiers, Henry Jermyn, 1st Earl of St Albans (1605-84), suspected of being the lover of Charles I's widow Henrietta Maria and perhaps even the father of Charles II. Hence we have **Jermyn Street**. Jermyn's grand design for St James's inspired the development of London's West End and he has gone down in history as the 'Father of the West End'.

* There are some wonderfully named little streets and alleyways off the main streets of St James's. **Pickering Place**, home of the Texan Embassy from 1842 to 1845, after which the Republic of Texas became part of the United States, was named after the man who built it in 1730, William Pickering, and is said to be the last place in London where a duel was fought. **Apple Tree Yard** is the site of the palace orchard and found fame as the title and setting of a 2017 BBC psychological thriller by Louise Doughty. There is a modern statue set into a niche in the building at the entrance to the yard commemorating the architect Edwin Lutyens, who had his office in Apple Tree Yard, and it was here that he worked on the designs for the Viceroy's House, now the Presidential Palace, in New Delhi in India. **Mason's Yard** was originally a stable yard named after Henry Mason, an eighteenth-century victualler whose premises backed on to the yard where he had his own stables. The short-lived Indica Gallery at No. 6 put on a show of Yoko Ono's work in 1966 where she first met John Lennon. Behind the green door at No. 13 is the Scotch of St James nightclub where a couple of months before, in September 1966, Jimi Hendrix gave his first performance in England and met his girlfriend Kathy Etchingham. **Ryder Street** and **Ryder Court** were named after Captain Richard Rider, master carpenter to Charles II.

* **Regent Street**. Begun in 1811 during the regency of the future George IV, Regent Street was laid out by architect John Nash to link the Prince Regent's palace at Carlton House with Marylebone Park, which was then renamed Regent's Park. At the heart of one of London's first planned developments, Regent Street quickly became one of the city's most fashionable shopping streets, and in 1850 was the first shopping centre in Britain to introduce late-night shopping, with the shops staying open until 7pm. Major stores on the street have included the mock-Tudor Liberty's; Hamleys, advertised as the world's largest toy shop; Jaeger, where Henry Morton Stanley bought the coat he wore in his encounter with 'Dr Livingstone, I presume?' and where Captain Scott of the Antarctic bought the coat he took to the South Pole; and the first Apple Store in Europe. The BBC headquarters and news centre, Broadcasting House, stands at the top of Regent Street next to the only building designed by John Nash that survives on the street, All Souls Church. **Hanover Street** leads from Regent Street to **Hanover Square**, laid out in 1717 in honour of the accession to the throne of the Elector of Hanover as George I in 1714.

* **Rotten Row**. The name of this broad avenue in Hyde Park is a corruption of the French *Rue du Roi*, meaning 'Road of the King'. It was laid out for William III as a safe route from St James's Palace (see page 140) to his home at Kensington Palace, which was then deep in the country. In 1690, as a precaution against the ever-present highway robbers, the avenue was lit with three hundred oil lamps, the first artificially lit street in Britain.

* **Savage Gardens**. The street takes its name from Sir Thomas Savage, who lived near here in the 1620s. He was an English peer and courtier in the court of Charles I and apparently had nineteen children.

MANCHESTER

* **Albert Square**. Laid out on derelict land in 1863 to showcase a
  memorial to Queen Victoria's husband Prince Albert, who had died
  of typhoid two years earlier in 1861, Albert Square is Manchester's
  centrepiece. The whole east side of the square is taken up with
  Manchester's gargantuan town hall, designed by Alfred Waterhouse
  in 1868 and one of the largest and finest Victorian neo-Gothic
  buildings in the world. The clock tower, 280 feet high, is one of the
  tallest buildings in Manchester and contains a set of bells that ring
  out with the same chime as Big Ben. Every year Albert Square hosts
  one of Britain's oldest and largest Christmas markets. Perhaps the
  most famous Albert Square of them all is the fictional Albert Square
  where the BBC soap opera *Eastenders* is set. The programme's
  producers chose the name on learning of Prince Albert's tireless
  work to improve the living and working conditions of London's
  East End. There is a real Albert Square in east London, in Stratford
  near the Olympic Park, although the Eastenders who live there are
  adamant that life in the real Albert Square is nothing like how it is
  depicted in the TV series.

* **Coronation Street**. Probably the most famous street name in
  Britain as the title of the world's longest-running TV soap opera,
  the Manchester-based *Coronation Street* was originally going
  to be called *Florizel Street* after the prince in 'Sleeping Beauty'.
  Fortunately for the show's legions of fans, a tea lady at Granada
  Studios said that Florizel sounded like a disinfectant and so the title
  was changed to something a little more conventional. Since the
  houses on the fictional Coronation Street were meant to have been
  built at the start of the twentieth century, the coronation referred
  to in the name is that of Edward VII in 1902. There are some
  eighty-seven real-life Coronation Streets in the UK according to the

Ordnance Survey database (as well as 171 instances of **Coronation Road**, ninety-three of **Coronation Avenue**, eight of **Coronation Square** and two of **Coronation Mews**), many of them late Victorian or Edwardian terraced streets, so it is likely that a lot of them also celebrate the coronation of Edward VII. There was also a building boom after the Second World War at the time of the coronation of Elizabeth II, and many Coronation Streets were named in honour of that occasion, too. You can fairly accurately guess at which coronation is being celebrated by the age of the houses in the street. Needless to say, there are no Florizel Streets in Britain.

* **King Street**. Manchester was one of the few towns to have a large and loyal Jacobite community, and this street was originally called James Square in honour of James II. It was renamed, ostensibly in honour of George I, after the defeat of Bonnie Prince Charlie at Culloden in 1745, although it may be that the Jacobites were secretly actually honouring King James III.

* **Kingsway**. A major dual carriageway built in 1928 to link the city centre to the southern suburbs, Kingsway was named in honour of King George V, who was on the throne at the time.

YORK

* **Coney Street**. Corruption of the Viking *konungr*, meaning 'king', this was originally Koningstreta or Cuningstreta - King's Street - and presumably refers to the Danish king Canute.

* **Goodramgate**. Thought to be named after the Viking king Guthrum who led the Danes to defeat against King Alfred at the Battle of Edington in 878 but ruled the subsequent Danelaw (the part of eastern England governed by the Danes) from York.

* **King's Staith**. 'King's landing place' on the north bank of the river Ouse. 'Staith' is based on a Viking word for 'quay'.

11

NOBLE
LANDOWNING
FAMILIES

It was during the eighteenth century that street names really began to proliferate. The Industrial Revolution saw people begin to move off the land and into the towns and cities, which had to expand rapidly to accommodate them. As the number of streets multiplied, so it became necessary to identify those streets by name, and it made sense to use the names of those who owned the land or the houses. During the eighteenth and much of the nineteenth century London expanded faster and further than any other city on Earth, and it has many examples of areas named after a landowner's family name, title or country estate.

BERKELEYS

Named after the 1st Lord Berkeley of Stratton, **Berkeley Square** in London began life as part of the garden of Berkeley House, a vast mansion overlooking Piccadilly that was built in 1662. The square was laid out in the 1730s and a row of houses built along the east and west sides some ten years later. Those on the east side have long gone, with much of the east side occupied by the world's biggest and oldest Bentley dealership, established in 1927 by Jack Barclay, one of the 'Bentley Boys' who raced the all-conquering Bentley sports cars at Brooklands and Le Mans in the 1920s.

The original terrace of houses survives along the west side and includes some of the finest Georgian properties in London. No. 44, built in 1742 by William Kent for Lady Isabella Finch, maid of honour to George II's daughter Princess Amelia, was thought by the influential architectural historian Nikolaus Pevsner to be the most perfect example of a terraced house in London. The modest exterior hides a magnificent staircase regarded as William Kent's masterpiece - it was described by Horace Walpole, who lived across the square at No. 11, 'as beautiful a piece of scenery and, considering the space, of art as can be imagined'. The house is now occupied by the aristocratic gambling establishment the Clermont Club, named after the Earl of Clermont, a previous owner, and founded by John Aspinall in 1962. Frequented by the hugely rich and famous - including dukes and prime ministers and the likes of Ian Fleming, Peter Sellers, Lucien Freud and Lord Lucan - it was around the flush gambling tables of the Clermont Club that private equity investment was conceived. The celebrated nightclub Annabel's occupies the basement.

Clive of India lived at No. 45 and committed suicide there in 1774. No. 50, where George Canning, Britain's shortest-serving prime minister lived, is reputed to be the most haunted house in London, the attic possessed by a brown mist containing the spirit of a young woman who committed suicide there in the mid-nineteenth century.

The plane trees in the gardens of Berkeley Square, many of them dating from 1789, are regarded as the finest in London with one, on the east side, recognised by the Capital Asset Valuation for Amenity Trees in 2008 as the most valuable street tree in Britain, worth an astonishing £750,000. (It has recently been overtaken by a plane tree in a churchyard in Islington, north London, valued at £1.6 million.)

In 1940 Berkeley Square achieved worldwide prominence thanks to a song made famous by Dame Vera Lynn, the Glenn Miller Band, Bing Crosby, Frank Sinatra and others: 'A Nightingale Sang in Berkeley Square'.

While Berkeley Square in London is named after a cadet branch of the Berkeley family, of the village of Berkeley in Gloucestershire, Berkeley Square in Bristol is named after the senior branch of the family, owners of Berkeley Castle, where Edward II was murdered in 1327. Heavily involved in the history of Bristol over the centuries, as founders of St Augustine's Abbey, which became Bristol Cathedral, the Berkeleys are the only English family still in existence that can trace their ancestry unbroken from father to son back to Saxon times, while Berkeley Castle is the oldest home in the country still to be owned and occupied by the family who originally built it. The first Berkeley was a Flemish nobleman called Roger de Tosny, who changed his name to Roger de Berkeley when granted the manor of Berkeley by William the Conqueror. Thus the family took their name from the village of Berkeley, its name derived from the Old English *berclea*, meaning 'birch lea'. And so Berkeley Square, in the very urban settings of Bristol and London, derives its name in each case from a bucolic grove of birch trees. In 1112 one of the younger Berkeleys went to Scotland with the Conqueror's great-niece Maud for her marriage to the Scottish king David I, and settled there. Six hundred years later, his descendant James Berkeley, now spelled 'Barclay', returned south and founded what became Barclays Bank.

DUKES OF GRAFTON

Euston Road takes is name from Euston Hall, the family seat in Suffolk of the Dukes of Grafton, who owned land to the west of London and wanted a road along which they could drive their cattle to Smithfield Market, avoiding the congestion of Oxford Street and Holborn.

And so in 1756 they built what was originally known as the New Road, effectively London's first bypass, which ran from Marylebone in the west to the City at Moorgate via the Angel, Islington (see page 103). The Dukes of Grafton began buying up land along the New Road and the Euston name was first used in the 1810s for **Euston Grove**, a rural lane that ran north from the New Road through nurseries and gardens. Next came **Euston Square**, completed in 1827 and the first serious development north of the New Road, which until then had served as the northern boundary of the London metropolis.

In 1837 Euston Station (then known as Euston Grove station) was opened on the site of Euston Grove. This was London's first mainline railway station, the terminus for the London and Birmingham Railway, and was designed by Robert Stephenson, inventor of the world's first practical steam locomotive, the Rocket. Until 1844 the steam engines were not powerful enough to climb the steep slope to the next station at Chalk Farm and so the passenger carriages had to be hauled up there by a rope attached to a fixed winding cable powered by a stationary steam engine, before being attached to the engine for the journey to Birmingham. Trains coming into London were detached from their engines at Chalk Farm and allowed to coast down the hill into Euston under their own weight, controlled by a brakeman. By 1850 Euston Station had become the grandest station in the world, the concourse a magnificent Great Hall with a sweeping double staircase fronted by a spectacular seventy-foot-high portico with Doric columns designed by Philip Hardwick that became known as the Euston Arch. It was demolished when the station was rebuilt in the 1960s in a move described by the *Architectural Review* as 'wanton and unnecessary', and its destruction sparked into life the modern conservation movement.

The section of the New Road from Marylebone to King's Cross was renamed the Euston Road in 1857 and the whole area has since taken the Euston name. Among the other properties in the area are **Euston Street**, the 400-foot-high Euston Tower, the Euston underpass and the Euston Square underground station. St Pancras railway station, King's Cross station and the British Library are all situated on the Euston Road.

DUKES OF NORTHUMBERLAND

Northumberland Avenue is a fine example of a street named after a noble landowning family. It is also a fine example of an urban avenue, wide and lined with trees. The avenue was laid out in 1874 on the site of a large country house built in 1609 for the Earl of Northampton and originally called Northampton House. When Northampton died, the house became the property of the Earl of Suffolk whose daughter married the Earl of Northumberland, thus becoming the Countess of Northumberland and turning Northampton House, as part of her dowry, into Northumberland House. The street upon which the house stood, some of which survives, was named **Northumberland Street**. By the 1870s the area had become very built up and the Northumberlands sold their house to the Metropolitan Board of Works, who demolished it to make way for a broad avenue of large hotels, namely the Grand, the Metropole and the Victoria, three of London's grandest Victorian establishments. The avenue is now a rather nondescript mixture of hotels, clubs and government offices. At the junction of Northumberland Avenue and Northumberland Street is a Victorian pub called the Sherlock Holmes, which began life as a small hotel, called the Northumberland Hotel, and then became the Northumberland Arms. An upstairs room has been transformed into a recreation of Sherlock Holmes's study and sitting room at 221b Baker Street and the walls are covered in Sherlock Holmes memorabilia, all collected together for an exhibition at Abbey House at 221 Baker Street (see page 159) during the Festival of Britain in 1951. The pub was chosen as the home for a permanent exhibition as Northumberland Avenue and its environs are featured in a number of the Sherlock Holmes stories. The Northumberland Hotel appears in the most famous of all the stories, *The Hound of the Baskervilles.* Sir Henry Baskerville, last of the Baskervilles, stays at the hotel when he arrives in London from Canada to claim his inheritance. It is here that he receives a letter, addressed to Sir Henry Baskerville, Northumberland Hotel, warning him, 'As you value your life or your reason, keep away from the moor.' And the Turkish baths frequented by Holmes and Watson were at No. 25 Northumberland Avenue, right next door to the pub. A couple of Turkish-style windows and a dab of oriental paintwork in Craven Passage (see page 110) beside the pub are the only indications that here was the location of the Nevill Turkish baths, one of several owned by Henry and James Forder Nevill.

GROSVENORS

Possibly the wealthiest landowners of all are the Grosvenors, Dukes of Westminster, who seem to be the landowners of London's most exclusive areas. They give their name to **Grosvenor Square** and **Grosvenor Street** in Mayfair, itself named after the fifteen-day May fair that was held here every year from the mid-seventeenth to the mid-eighteenth century, and **Grosvenor Place** in Belgravia, itself named after one of their titles, Viscount Belgrave, based on the name of a village they own in Cheshire. Also in Belgravia is **Belgrave Square, Eaton Square** - named for their country home in Cheshire, Eaton Hall - and **Eccleston Street**, from the Cheshire village of Eccleston where the Dukes of Westminster are traditionally buried.

PORTMANS AND PORTLANDS

The streets of Marylebone are predominantly called after the family names and estates of local landowners, the major landowners being the Portman family and the Dukes of Portland.

In 1533 Sir William Portman, Lord Chief Justice of England, purchased two hundred acres of land in and around Marylebone and in the eighteenth century his descendants started to develop it, beginning with **Portman Square**, at one time London's most exclusive square. The Portmans came from Orchard Portman in Somerset, hence **Orchard Street**, and also owned a lot of land around Blandford Forum in Dorset, hence **Blandford Street** and **Dorset Street**, in addition to **Clenston Mews**, from the village of Winterbourne Clenston, and **Crawford Street**, from Tarrant Crawford, both Dorset villages where the Portmans had land.

The Dukes of Portland, of the Isle of Portland in Dorset, give us: **Portland Place** and **Great Portland Street**; **Bingham Place** from their lands around Bingham in Nottinghamshire; **Bryanston Square** from their lands in Bryanston in Dorset; **Welbeck Street** from Welbeck Abbey in Nottinghamshire, seat of the 2nd Duke of Portland; **Weymouth Street** from his daughter Viscountess Weymouth; and **Bentinck Street** from the Portland's family name - they were originally a Dutch family who came over to England with the Dutch king William of Orange (William III). The Dukes of Portland were related by marriage to the Cavendish family, Dukes of Devonshire, hence **Devonshire Place**, **Devonshire Street** and **Cavendish Square**, and to Edward Harley, 2nd Earl of Oxford, from whom we get **Harley Street**, famous as the home of numerous expensive private medical and dental practices. Also **Wigmore Street**, after the earl's country seat of Wigmore Castle in Herefordshire, and **Wimpole Street**, home of the Barretts of Wimpole Street, named after another of the earl's country seats, Wimpole Hall in Cambridgeshire.

OTHER FAMILIES

BROWN CONSTABLE STREET, DUNDEE

Running through an area of mixed Victorian and modern housing blocks and disused factories, Brown Constable Street is named after the landowner Colonel Charles Brown Constable (1807-87). The site was once occupied by a country house known as Wallace Craigie, home of Brown Constable's ancestor George Constable, a friend of Sir Walter Scott and on whom the writer based Jonathan Oldbuck, the leading character from his novel *The Antiquary*.

CAMP HILL, BIRMINGHAM

Named after the Kempe family, who are recorded as having a farm here as far back as the 1350s. The Battle of Camp Hill was fought here in 1643 during the English Civil War by Parliamentarians and local people who were trying to prevent the Royalist troops under the command of Prince Rupert from passing through the area.

COLMORE ROW, BIRMINGHAM

Named after a leading seventeenth-century textile-trading family, the Colmores. Nearby **Edmund Street** is named after Edmund Colmore, while **Newhall Street** was originally the driveway leading up to their house, New Hall.

DUKE STREET, GLASGOW

At over one and a half miles in length, Glasgow's Duke Street is one of the longest urban 'streets' in Britain. It takes its name from the 1st Duke of Montrose (1682-1742), who had a house on the street.

FINTRY ROAD AND FINTRY DRIVE, DUNDEE

These two roads run through Fintry, a post-war housing estate built on what was once the estate of the sixteenth-century Fintry Castle (now Mains Castle) on the north side of Dundee. Fintry was named after the Grahams of Fintry in Stirlingshire, who emigrated to South Africa in the nineteenth century and founded Grahamstown on the Eastern Cape.

LOWTHER STREET, WHITEHAVEN, CUMBRIA

Lowther Street, the main street at the centre of a grid of Georgian streets that inspired the grid system of New York, was laid out in the eighteenth century by local landowners the Lowther family, Earls of Lonsdale.

MARISCHAL STREET, ABERDEEN

Named after the Earl Marischal's Hall, which was demolished to make way for the street in 1789. The first planned street in Aberdeen and the first to be paved with granite, it also became Aberdeen's first bridged street when **Bannerman's Bridge** (named after the builder and stone mason Alex Bannerman) was built across **Virginia Street** (named after Aberdeen's expanding trade with Virginia in America) in 1768 to allow Marischal Street to slope gradually down to the harbour. The role of the Earl Marischal is to guard the royal regalia of Scotland and it is a hereditary office held since the twelfth century by the head of Clan Keith. At the end of the street sits the Marischal College, the largest granite building in the world after the Escorial in Madrid.

MOSLEY STREET, MANCHESTER

Named after seventeenth-century landowner Nicholas Mosley, who purchased the manor of Manchester in 1596.

PERCY STREET, NEWCASTLE UPON TYNE

Taken from 'Percy', the family name of local landowners the Dukes of Northumberland. **Neville Street** is likewise so called after the family name of the Earls of Westmorland, whose townhouse, Westmorland Place, stood on the site in medieval times.

POWELL STREET, ABERYSTWYTH

Powell Street, **Laura Place**, **George Street** and **William Street** are all named after members of the landowning Powell family of nearby Nanteos Mansion - said by some to have been the hiding place for centuries of the Holy Grail, a wooden drinking bowl supposedly fashioned from a piece of wood from the True Cross, that was carried here by monks fleeing Glastonbury Abbey after Henry VIII's dissolution of the monasteries. The Grail is believed to have been brought to Glastonbury originally by Joseph of Arimathea, who had charged the monks there to guard it with their lives.

12

BUILDERS AND DEVELOPERS

BAKER STREET, LONDON

Baker Street in London is named after the man who laid it out in 1755, builder William Baker. Originally an upmarket residential street, it is now a classic urban street with shops and offices lining both sides of the road and houses towards the northern end. The street and, thus, William Baker give their name to the world's oldest underground railway station, Baker Street Station, and to the Baker Street and Waterloo Railway, now known as the Bakerloo Line on the London Underground. Baker Street's most famous resident – and the reason why people come from all over the world to see it – is, of course, Sir Arthur Conan Doyle's detective Sherlock Holmes, who lived at 221b. This actual address did not exist when the books were written and would have been in what was then called Upper Baker Street, but when Baker Street was extended and renumbered in the 1930s, 221 became part of the address for the headquarters of the Abbey Road Building Society, which later became the Abbey National. Until it moved from Baker Street in 2005, Abbey National employed a full-time secretary to answer letters addressed to Sherlock Holmes. In 1990 the Sherlock Holmes Museum opened at No. 239 Baker Street in a house very similar to that described in the Sherlock Holmes books, and the museum obtained special permission from the Post Office to change the address to 221b. Baker Street is also known to a worldwide audience thanks to the 1978 song 'Baker Street', famous for its saxophone riff, that was written by Gerry Rafferty while he was staying in a friend's flat just off the street.

BEATRICE ROAD, LEICESTER

An area of Victorian terraces named after Beatrice Harrison, who sold the land to builder Orson Wright on the condition that he named the streets after her family. Hence the streets running into Beatrice Road are **Hawthorne Street**, **Alma Street**, **Rowan Street**, **Ruby**

Street, **Ivanhoe Street**, **Sylvan Street**, **Oban Street** and **Newport Street**, their first letters forming the name 'Harrison'.

DOWNING STREET, LONDON

The most famous street in Britain and home to No. 10, the most famous address in Britain, Downing Street has become a metonym for the prime minister and the executive in Britain.

Like so many streets, Downing Street gets its name from the man who built it, Sir George Downing (1624-84), diplomat, statesman, the second person ever to graduate from Harvard University and, fittingly enough, politician.

In 1682 Downing obtained the lease of land on the site of what had been a large mansion called Hampden House, and built a cul de sac of fifteen to twenty inexpensive brick terraced houses on the site, modestly naming the street after himself. Downing was something of what we might call in modern parlance a 'spiv', described by his clerk Samuel Pepys as a 'perfidious rogue', and although Sir Christopher Wren was commissioned to design the houses, and he did not come cheap, they were shoddily built with shallow foundations on unstable ground, and even had to have mortar lines drawn on to the facades to make them look more substantial. As one distinguished occupant, Winston Churchill, put it, the Downing Street houses were 'shaky and lightly built by the profiteering contractor whose name they bear'.

In 1732 George II bought part of No. 10 and offered it to his first minister, Sir Robert Walpole, the first person to be known as 'prime minister', as a gift for services to his country. Walpole accepted the house, not to live in but to serve as the office of the First Lord of the Treasury, and this, according to the inscription on the brass letterbox of the celebrated front door, is technically what No. 10 still is, as the title is held to this day by the prime minister.

More famous people, including world leaders, film stars, statesmen and royalty, have walked up Downing Street than any other street in the world and that 'profiteering contractor' Sir George Downing has profited in ways he could never have dreamed of, his name recognised across the entire planet. Intriguingly, Sir George Downing also has a street named after him in Greenwich Village in New York, spookily enough right next to Sir Winston Churchill Square. Downing was responsible for arranging the handover of New Amsterdam to the British in 1664, at which point it became New York.

After all that, the Downing Street in London isn't really a street at all. Not, as you might think, because there is no public right of way, something that a street, by definition, must have, as we have discussed elsewhere. Before 1990 anyone could walk right up to the famous door of No. 10 and have their photo taken, but the rise of terrorism in the 1980s, mainly by the IRA, forced the authorities to put a large iron gate across the entrance to the street and restrict access. However, the public right of way along Downing Street has not actually been removed, only suspended, and the road remains technically a public highway. Public access was restricted through common law powers designed to prevent a breach of the peace, a decision later formalised under anti-terrorism laws. No, the reason Downing Street should not really qualify as a street is that, although it has buildings along both sides, it has no vehicular access at one end, merely a set of steps, so it's really more of a close. And when it was built in the 1680s, Downing Street was actually a cul de sac with houses at the western end, where the steps are now. Somehow, though, Downing End doesn't have quite the same ring to it.

GRAINGER STREET, NEWCASTLE UPON TYNE

Named after developer Richard Grainger (1797-1861), who redeveloped a hundred acres of the centre of Newcastle in fine 'Tyneside Classical' style between 1824 and 1841. The area is now known as Grainger Town.

LEMON STREET, TRURO

Named after a local merchant and MP for Cornwall, Sir William Lemon, who built houses along the street at the start of the nineteenth century.

PENTONVILLE ROAD, LONDON

Pentonville Road is a rare example of a street that is not a High Street or a Main Street but nonetheless takes its name from the area it runs through, in this case Pentonville, laid out in 1773 as one of London's first planned suburbs by the MP for Winchester, Henry Penton. Pentonville itself was an example of ribbon development, running for almost a mile alongside what was then the easternmost section of the New Road, between Marylebone and the Angel, Islington (named after the Angel Inn at Islington), but only a few streets deep to either side. The road was renamed Pentonville Road in 1857 at the same time as the adjoining section of the New Road to the west was renamed Euston Road.

Henry Penton naturally named the smartest street in Pentonville after himself, **Penton Street**, which runs north off Pentonville Road.

There are no other Pentonville Roads in Britain, making it unique. There *is* a road called simply **Pentonville** in Newport in Wales, upon which stands the former Shire Hall. The land was owned by Lord Tredegar, who had holdings not far from Pentonville in London and for this reason possibly named his Newport street after the original Pentonville.

13

LOCAL WORTHIES, INDUSTRIALISTS, INVENTORS AND PHILANTHROPISTS

BIRMINGHAM

* **Brindley Place**. Astonishingly, Birmingham has more miles of canal than Venice, a legacy of its industrial past. Brindley Place borders the Birmingham Canal, which runs from Birmingham to Wolverhampton and is named after the canal engineer James Brindley (1716-72), who built not only this canal but Britain's first modern-era canal, the Bridgewater Canal in Manchester.

* **Jennens Road**. Named after the Jennens family, ironmongers in the seventeenth century. The last of the family died in 1798, leaving a fortune of £12 million that has never been claimed. It is believed that Charles Dickens based Jarndyce and Jarndyce, the interminable legal case over wills in *Bleak House*, on the Jennens.

DUNDEE

Dundee is famous for jute, jam and journalism and this is reflected in a number of its street names.

Jute is a strong textile used for making sacks, rope and matting and it was a major Dundee industry in the nineteenth century. Now cheaper to produce in India, the last jute mill in Dundee closed in the 1970s. **Caird Avenue** and **Caird Terrace** honour Dundee-born jute baron Sir James Caird (1837-1916), while **Malcolm Street** and **Ogilvie Street** remember Malcolm Ogilvie & Co., one of the last Dundee jute manufacturers.

Jam, in this instance, means marmalade, which was first produced for sale in Dundee in 1797 by shopkeeper Janet Keiller, whose son James had brought back from Spain a cargo of bitter Seville oranges. She boiled the oranges up with sugar to make marmalade and the recipe proved so popular that James later founded a company, James Keiller & Son, to produce Keiller's Dundee Marmalade - the first commercially made marmalade in the world. Throughout the nineteenth century, James Keiller & Son was the world's largest producer of marmalade. The Keiller Shopping Centre in Dundee is named in its honour.

Journalism refers to D. C. Thomson & Co., publishers of the *Dundee Courier* and popular comics *The Beano* and *The Dandy*. In 2014 a street in Dundee was named **Bash Street** after the Bash Street Kids, the anarchic schoolchildren from *The Beano*. The characters were created in 1953 by Leo Baxendale, inspired by the children pouring out of Dundee High School into the playground, which is overlooked by the publishers' offices.

* **Fleming Gardens**. A street running through the Fleming Gardens Estate, located in the hills north of Dundee. The estate was financed by Dundee-born banker Robert Fleming (1845-1933), who wanted to improve the quality of housing for Dundee's workers. Fleming had formed Robert Fleming & Co. merchant bank in 1873 and made much of his fortune by investing in American railways. He is the grandfather of James Bond creator Ian Fleming.

* **Tindal's Wynd**. Not much is left of Dundee's oldest street, one of the city's many 'wynds' (see page 42). It was laid down in the twelfth century to give access to the castle from the waterfront and was then known, appropriately enough, as Castle Wynd. In the early fourteenth century, a prominent merchant called Alexander Skirling lived in a house on the street, and the name was changed to Skirling's Wynd. The current name refers to another resident of the street, David Tyndal, who was a baker and town councillor in the sixteenth century. Interestingly, the first person recorded as living in the wynd, in 1270, when it was still Castle Wynd, was an official who went by the unfortunate name of Rodger de Vend or Rodger of the Wynd.

GLASGOW

In the eighteenth and nineteenth centuries, Glasgow was known as the Second City of the Empire and many of the streets were named after the city's industries and Glasgow's industrial barons of the time. **Buchanan Street** was named after tobacco merchant Andrew Buchanan, head of two Virginia tobacco houses. **Jamaica Street** was named in reference to Glasgow's rum and sugar trade with Jamaica. **Bath Street** takes its name from the public baths built there in the early 1800s by the 'water entrepreneur' and gingham manufacturer William Harley. **Bartholomew Street** was named for cotton trader John Bartholomew of Cotton Hall. **Charles Street** and **Tennant Street** were named for Charles Tennant, inventor of bleaching powder, who set up the world's largest chemical works at St Rollox in Glasgow in 1800. **Saracen Street** was named after the Saracen foundry of Walter Macfarlane & Co., Scotland's leading manufacturer of ornamental ironwork. **Warroch Street** was named after the brewery of Murdoch, Warroch & Co., the first brewery in Glasgow to brew porter, in 1775. King George III stated that George Murdoch, the senior partner in the brewery, was 'the handsomest Scotsman he had ever seen'. **Macintosh Street** was named for George Macintosh, owner of a tanning and dye works that stood on the site. His son Charles invented the Macintosh waterproof coat, which was first sold in 1824. Another inventor is recalled in **James Watt Street**, named after Watt's House, which stood on this site until 1849 and was the one-time workshop of the man who invented the practical steam engine after a flash of inspiration - the separate condenser - while walking across Glasgow Green in 1765.

LONDON

* **Beech Street**, City of London. Named after Nicholas de la Beche, a lieutenant at the Tower of London during the reign of Edward III.

* **George Peabody Street**, Plaistow. A familiar name in London, George Peabody (1795-1869) was an American financier and founder of J. P. Morgan & Co. who is regarded as the 'Father of Modern Philanthropy'. In 1862 he founded the Peabody Trust to provide housing for the 'artisans and labouring poor of London', and Peabody estates can be found all across the capital. This street honouring his memory is part of a recent Peabody development on the site of the former Plaistow Hospital.

MANCHESTER

* **John Dalton Street**. Named after the 'Father of Modern Atomic Theory', chemist and physicist John Dalton (1766-1844), whose experiments in his laboratory at Manchester Literary and Philosophical Society concluded that all matter is made up of atoms. Dalton's atomic theory, put forward in 1803, was one of the most important scientific breakthroughs in history and placed Manchester at the forefront of scientific discovery, a position later enhanced by Ernest Rutherford's discoveries at Manchester University in the 1920s (see below).

* **Radium Street**, Ancoats, Manchester. Named in recognition of Ernest Rutherford's work on radium at Manchester University.

* **Simonsway**, Wythenshawe. Named after German-born engineer Henry Simon (1835-99), who came to live in Manchester in 1860 and invented a rolling flour-milling process for McDougall Brothers which transformed flour milling, as well as a new, less toxic means of manufacturing coke. Along with the Anglo-German pianist and conductor Charles Hallé, he founded Manchester's famous Hallé Orchestra. He also helped establish the Manchester Physics Laboratories as the birthplace of modern nuclear physics, where Ernest Rutherford and his team discovered the proton and first

produced a nuclear reaction. In 1926 his son, the 1st Baron Simon of Wythenshawe, purchased the sixteenth-century Wythenshawe Hall on the south-western edge of Manchester and donated the estate to Manchester Corporation, where they built what was then Europe's largest council estate.

* **Whitworth Street**. Named after the engineer and philanthropist Joseph Whitworth (1803-87), creator of the British Standard Whitworth system for screw threads and the Whitworth rifle, whose works formerly lined the street.

NEWCASTLE UPON TYNE

The centre of Newcastle, which was redeveloped in the nineteenth century, has a number of streets named after local worthies. **Stowell Street** is named after John Scott, Baron Stowell (1745-1836), who became Lord Chancellor of England. He was famed in Newcastle for eloping with banker's daughter Bessie Surtees, helping her climb down a ladder from her bedroom in Newcastle's finest surviving Jacobean house down on the riverfront at the bottom of Grey Street, and then escaping over the Scottish border to get married in Blackshields. **Worswick Street** is named after the Reverend James Worswick (1771-1843), who founded the first Roman Catholic church to be built in Newcastle after the Reformation. **Blackett Street** is named for John Blackett (1728-1814), who was several times mayor of Newcastle during the late eighteenth century. **Clayton Street** is named after John Clayton (1792-1890), town clerk and antiquarian responsible for masterminding the redevelopment of the city centre. **John Dobson Street** is named after architect John Dobson (1787-1865), who designed Newcastle Central Station. **Hood Street** is named after John Hood (1799-1848), mayor of Newcastle for ten years between 1825 and 1835.

Mosley Street recalls the name of another mayor of Newcastle, Edward Mosley, who held the post three times, in 1767, 1773 and 1781. A century later, in 1881, Mosley Street became the first street in the world to be lit by electric light bulbs, invented and installed by Joseph Swan from Gateshead and supplied from the world's first light bulb factory at Benwell in Newcastle, which had been opened by Swan earlier that same year. Swan first demonstrated his light bulb at the Newcastle Literary and Philosophical Society on 3 February 1879, ten months before Thomas Edison in America.

NOTTINGHAM

* **Carrington Street**. Named in honour of philanthropic banker and MP for Nottingham Robert Smith, 1st Baron Carrington (1752-1838), whose family built hospitals and alms houses in Nottingham. Carrington is a suburb of Nottingham.

* **Jesse Boot Avenue**. Named after Nottingham-born chemist Jesse Boot (1850-1931), who turned his father's chemist shop in Nottingham into one of the world's leading pharmacy chains, Boots the Chemist.

OTHER TOWNS AND CITIES

* **Babbage Road**, Totnes, Devon. Named in honour of Charles Babbage (1791-1871), known as the 'Father of Computers' for his invention of what many regard as the first computer, the Analytical Engine, which contained all the essential components of the modern computer. He lived as a boy in Teignmouth in Devon and went to school in Totnes, where his image appeared on the local currency, the Totnes pound, in circulation from 2007 to 2019.

* **Geoffrey Road**, Norwich. Named after Geoffrey Colman (1892-1935), a member of the famous Norwich Colman's Mustard family. Something of an eccentric, he drove around the city in a

carriage drawn by goats and did numerous philanthropic works for the people of Norwich, as well as being a first-class cricketer.

* **George Hudson Street**, York. Born in Howsham near York, George Hudson (1800-1871) was a major financier and promoter of the railways, particularly those joining London to Edinburgh, who became known as the Railway King. Twice Lord Mayor of York, he helped the city become the major railway hub it is today.

* **George Stephenson Boulevard**, Stockton-on-Tees. This street and **George Stephenson Drive** in Darlington remember the 'Father of the Railways' George Stephenson (1781-1848), who built the world's first passenger railway line, the Stockton and Darlington Railway.

* **Guild Street**, Aberdeen. The site of Aberdeen's main rail and bus stations, Guild Street was named after Scottish minister William Guild (1586-1657), chaplain to Charles I and son of Matthew Guild, a wealthy Aberdeen armourer and philanthropist. A popular fixture on the street, and dedicated to William Guild, is Fidler's Wallie, a drinking fountain erected by Alexander 'Sandy' Fidler in 1857. As a token of appreciation, the council gave Fidler a watch worth £20. The fountain cost £18.

* **Isaac Newton Way**, Grantham. Named in honour of the scientist who discovered gravity and invented the first reflecting telescope. He was born a few miles to the south of Grantham at Woolsthorpe Manor on Christmas Day 1643.

* **Mary Seacole Road**, Plymouth. Named for the Jamaican-born nurse Mary Seacole (1805-81), who did pioneering work during the Crimean War (1853-6). She was the first black woman to become a nurse in Britain.

* **Nile Court**, Ayr. Named in honour of Ayrshire-born James Templeton (1851-1906), who went off to Egypt, became a successful builder and sent some of his fortune home to Ayr to redevelop the town.

* **Rosalind Franklin Close**, Guildford. A street on a modern research park that honours Dr Rosalind Franklin (1920-1958), an X-ray crystallographer who played a vital role in working out the structure of DNA. Her pioneering work was key in directing the discovery in 1953 of the DNA double helix by James Watson, Francis Crick and Maurice Wilkins, for which they received a Nobel Prize in 1963, four years after Dr Franklin had died of cancer. Nearby is **Francis Crick Road**. Also nearby is **Alan Turing Road**, named after the cryptologist who cracked the Enigma code at Bletchley Park in the Second World War. His code-breaking machine is considered one of the first practical modern computers.

* **Sir Thomas Street**, Liverpool. Named for Sir Thomas Johnson (1664-1728), the first mayor of Liverpool after the town had received its charter in 1695.

* **Wolseley Street**, Belfast. Named after the Belfast-born inventor Frederick York Wolseley (1837-99), who went to Australia and, in 1887, invented a sheep-shearing machine that revolutionised sheep shearing across the world. He later went into car manufacturing, producing Wolseley Cars.

14

WRITERS, ARTISTS, MUSICIANS AND SPORTSMEN

As well as kings and queens, battles, notable worthies and politicians, the Victorians added writers and artists to the list of people to be honoured with streets named after them. Musicians and sportspeople came along a little later – there were few really major British composers before the latter part of the nineteenth century and professional sport was in its infancy. Many street names recall artists and writers that have a connection to the area, although twentieth-century housing estates tend to name their streets after a trending theme or group, regardless of any connection. It is rare for a street to be named after a living person, but it happens.

WRITERS

ADDISON ROAD, KENSINGTON, LONDON

Along with **Addison Avenue**, **Crescent**, **Gardens** and **Place**, Addison Road was named for the writer and politician Joseph Addison (1672-1719), who lived at nearby Holland House in Holland Park, where he died. Along with his friend Richard Steele, Addison founded two eminent magazines, *The Tatler* in 1709 and *The Spectator* in 1711. Addison Road is today the second most expensive residential street in London. John Galsworthy (see page 177) lived at No. 14 from 1905 to 1913, and Chaim Weizmann, first President of Israel, lived at No. 67 from 1916 to 1919.

BUNYAN COURT, BARBICAN, LONDON

Named after John Bunyan (1628-88), author of the first English bestseller, *The Pilgrim's Progress*. He lived for a time in the area and attended St Giles-without-Cripplegate Church.

CAXTON STREET, WESTMINSTER, LONDON

Named after William Caxton (1422-91), not a writer as such but someone who helped writers sell rather more of their works by introducing the printing press into Britain and who became the first English retailer of printed books. The very first book he printed was Chaucer's *The Canterbury Tales* in 1476. On the street is Caxton Hall, once famous for its celebrity civil marriages. Included amongst those who were married there are world speed-record holder Donald Campbell, Diana Dors, Elizabeth Taylor (to Michael Wilding), Peter Sellars (his third marriage, to Miranda Quarry), Roger Moore, Joan Collins and Ringo Starr of the Beatles.

DEFOE ROAD, STOKE NEWINGTON, LONDON

Named after the author of *Robinson Crusoe*, Daniel Defoe (1660-1731), who lived here for a large part of his life. He is also remembered in the name of the Daniel Defoe pub, which stands nearby, and **Crusoe Mews**, a modern development a little to the north.

DICKENS ROAD, BROADSTAIRS, KENT

Commemorating the novelist Charles Dickens (1812-70), for whom Broadstairs was a favourite summer holiday destination. He famously lodged at Fort House, a huge crenellated mansion built on the site of the town's North Cliff Battery in 1801. It was while staying here that Dickens wrote *David Copperfield*. The road the house stands on is still called **Fort Road**, but after Dickens's death the house itself was renamed Bleak House in the author's honour after his novel of that name.

A road called **Copperfield Street**, in Borough, London, recalls the earlier novel, and there are other streets in the area named after characters from the writer's work. Dickens lived in Borough during the time that his father was imprisoned in the Marshalsea debtors' prison that stood nearby, itself remembered in **Marshalsea Road**. Other streets in the same area that commemorate characters in Dickens's novels are **Dorrit Street**, **Little Dorrit Court** and **Doyce**

Street (after the heroine, Little Dorrit, and the inventor Daniel Doyce in *Little Dorrit*), **Quilp Street** (after Daniel Quilp, the villain in *The Old Curiosity Shop*), **Trundle Street** and **Weller Street** (after Mr Trundle and Samuel Weller, Mr Pickwick's servant, in *Pickwick Papers*, Weller being one of Dickens's most popular characters).

EVELYN STREET, DEPTFORD, LONDON

Named after the seventeenth-century diarist John Evelyn, who owned a house, Sayes Court, in Deptford. He created one of the first formal English gardens there and in the nineteenth century his descendants offered it to the social reformer Octavia Hill as a public open space. This prompted Hill to set up the National Trust a few years later to preserve such open spaces for the public good, even though Sayes Court had by then already been given to the local authority, who let it go to ruin. Nearby is **Grinling Gibbons Place**, named after the matchless wood carver, who lived in a cottage in Deptford he rented from Evelyn and whom the diarist introduced to Charles II and Christopher Wren.

GALSWORTHY ROAD, KINGSTON UPON THAMES, SURREY

Home to Kingston Hospital, Galsworthy Road was named for the novelist we met on page 175 in Addison Road, John Galsworthy (1867-1933), who was born nearby at Parkhurst, now Galsworthy House Nursing Home, on Kingston Hill. His best-known work was the *Forsyte Saga*, which was dramatised as a hugely popular television series by the BBC in 1967 and as a new series by ITV in 2002. He won the Nobel Prize for Literature in 1932.

KEATS GROVE, HAMPSTEAD

Named for the Romantic poet John Keats (1795-1821), who lived in a house (now Keats House) on this road from 1818 to 1820. The mulberry tree under which he wrote 'Ode to a Nightingale' is still there in the garden where he would stroll with his love, Fanny Brawne. As Keats might have said, in reference to the long-lived tree or maybe to Fanny, 'A thing of beauty is a joy for ever'.

THE OCEAN AT THE END OF THE LANE, SOUTHSEA, PORTSMOUTH

Named in honour of the 2013 novel by Neil Gaiman, who was born in Portsmouth in 1960 and whose grandparents lived in Southsea.

ROALD DAHL PLASS, CARDIFF

Named after the ever-popular children's author, who was born in Cardiff in 1916, this public space stands right at the beating heart of Cardiff's redeveloped dockland between the Welsh Parliament (Senedd) and the Wales Millennium Centre for Performing Arts. Roald Dahl was born of Norwegian parents, hence the use of the Norwegian 'Plass' rather than Place or Square, and the Norwegian seafarers' church where Dahl was baptised stands close by.

STRATFORD ROAD, HEATON, NEWCASTLE UPON TYNE

No list of street names referring to writers would be complete, of course, without a nod to the Bard. Here, in a quiet corner of Newcastle is a collection of Victorian terraced streets honouring the memory of the great playwright - there was formerly an actual Shakespeare Road here but that, alas, got swept away when the area was partially redeveloped. To go with Stratford Road we do, however, have a **Warwick Street** - Shakespeare was born in Stratford-upon-Avon in Warwickshire and is buried there - and then four streets named after characters from his plays: **Bolingbroke Street** and **Mowbray Street** (*Richard II*); **Hotspur Street** (*Henry IV, Part I*); and **Malcolm Street** (*Macbeth*). Why Shakespeare? Apparently it was all at the suggestion of a nineteenth-century Shakespearean actor called George Stanley who lived in Heaton. And, although Shakespeare

Road may be no more, there is a **Shakespeare Street** in the city centre - appropriately enough, it runs along the south side of the Theatre Royal on Grey Street.

TENNIEL CLOSE, BAYSWATER, LONDON

Named in memory of illustrator Sir John Tenniel (1820-1914), principal cartoonist of *Punch* magazine for over fifty years and creator of ninety-two drawings for Lewis *Carroll's Alice in Wonderland* and *Through the Looking-Glass*, who was born in Bayswater.

WODEHOUSE PLACE, GUILDFORD

Comic writer P. G. Wodehouse (1881-1975), creator of the gormless Bertie Wooster and his trusty gentleman's gentleman, Jeeves, was born in his aunt's house at what was then 59 Epsom Road at the top of the High Street in Guildford. His parents lived in Hong Kong, but Wodehouse arrived prematurely while his mother was staying in Guildford with her sister. Shortly afterwards he was baptised Pelham Grenville in St Nicholas Church at the bottom of the High Street.

WORDSWORTH STREET, KESWICK

Named after William Wordsworth (1770-1850), one of the so-called Lake Poets who lived in the Lake District, in Wordsworth's case for over fifty years, during which time he wandered lonely as a cloud and his heart leapt up when he beheld a rainbow in the sky. The other Lake Poets were Samuel Taylor Coleridge (1772-1834), who is remembered in Keswick by **Coleridge Court**, and Robert Southey (1774-1843), in whose memory there is **Southey Street**.

MUSICIANS

GERRY RAFFERTY DRIVE, PAISLEY
Named in honour of the singer-songwriter Gerry Rafferty, who was born in Paisley in 1947. Founder member of the band Stealers Wheel, Rafferty features in an earlier chapter as the composer of the Ivor Novello award-winning No. 1 song 'Baker Street' (see page 159).

JOHN LENNON DRIVE, KENSINGTON, LIVERPOOL
Here we have a 1980s housing estate honouring Liverpool's most famous sons, the Beatles, and to that end there is also **Paul McCartney Way**, **George Harrison Close** and **Ringo Starr Drive**. **Epstein Court** remembers the Beatles' manager Brian Epstein and **Apple Court** their record label, while **Cavern Court** is named for the Liverpool nightclub where they began their career, the Cavern Club.

LIND ROAD, SUTTON, LONDON
Named in honour of the Swedish opera star Jenny Lind (1820-1887), who had arrived to great acclaim in London in 1847 just when Sutton was being redeveloped around its new train station. The pub on the corner of Lind Road and the road to Carshalton, **Carshalton Road**, is called the Nightingale after Jenny Lind's nickname, the 'Swedish Nightingale'; it was previously called the Jenny Lind.

RONNIE LANE, MANOR PARK, LONDON
This modern residential cul de sac is appropriately named after songwriter and bass guitarist Ronnie Lane (1946-97), who was born in nearby Plaistow. He was a founder member, along with Kenney Jones, of both Small Faces and Faces.

VAUGHAN WILLIAMS WAY, WARLEY, BRENTWOOD

A modern development with street names based around the English composer Ralph Vaughan Williams (1872-1958) and his works. In 1903 Vaughan Williams visited a school in Brentwood to give a talk about folk songs. While in Essex he heard about an elderly gardener in the nearby village of Ingrave, who was known to be knowledgeable about lost Essex folk songs, and went to visit him. The composer was spellbound by the beautiful melodies of the songs the gardener sang for him and came away inspired to write music that drew on the traditions of such songs. Vaughan Williams returned to the county many times to search for more forgotten folk songs and, sixty years after his death in 1958, Essex recognised his affection for the county by naming the streets of a new development after the works inspired by his first visit in 1903. Hence we have **Greensleeves Drive**, **Fantasia Court**, **Tallis Way**, **Drovers Mead**, **Lark Close** and **Potiphar Place**.

VERA LYNN CLOSE, FOREST GATE, LONDON

This modern close was named after Dame Vera Lynn (1917-2020), who was born just down the road from Vera Lynn Close, in East Ham. A popular singer who gave morale-boosting concerts for the troops in Egypt, Burma and India during the Second World War, she became affectionately known as the 'Forces' Sweetheart'. 'We'll Meet Again', 'A Nightingale Sang in Berkeley Square', 'There'll Always be an England' and 'There'll be Bluebirds Over the White Cliffs of Dover' are among the songs for which she will be best loved and remembered. Her compilation album *We'll Meet Again: The Very Best of Vera Lynn* reached No. 1 in the UK charts in 2009 when she was ninety-two, making her the oldest person ever to have a UK No. 1. In 2017 she released another album, *Vera Lynn 100*, to celebrate her hundredth birthday, and it reached No. 3 in the UK charts, making her the only centenarian ever to have a top-ten album.

ENTERTAINERS FROM THE STAGE AND SCREEN

ANNA NEAGLE CLOSE, FOREST GATE, LONDON

A modern close commemorating the actress and singer Dame Anna Neagle (1904-86), who was born nearby in Forest Gate. Renowned for playing historical figures such as Nell Gwyn, Queen Victoria, Nurse Edith Cavell and Florence Nightingale, she was voted Britain's most popular star in 1949.

AVENUE GRIMALDI, LUTON

Early Victorian street named in memory of the celebrated clown Joseph Grimaldi (1778-1837), pioneer of modern pantomime and the most popular entertainer of the Regency era. The *Illustrated London News* mourned his death in May 1837 with the words, 'Grimaldi is dead and hath left no peer. We fear with him the spirit of pantomime has disappeared.' He is buried in Joseph Grimaldi Park on Pentonville Road in London, which was created out of the graveyard of the former St James's Chapel, built in 1787 to serve Pentonville, but demolished in the 1980s to be replaced with an office building designed in the style of the original chapel. Also buried here are Grimaldi's patron, Charles Dibdin, proprietor of Sadler's Wells theatre, and Henry Penton, the founder of Pentonville, although their gravestones have been lost. As a tribute to Grimaldi, lying on the grass in one corner of the park are two coffin-shaped platforms made of bronze floor tiles which play musical notes when stepped upon - with the right sequence of steps it is possible to play Grimaldi's signature tune 'Hot Codlins'.

BAYLIS ROAD, LAMBETH, LONDON

Named after theatrical producer Lilian Baylis (1874-1937), who took over in 1912 from her aunt Emma Cons, first woman on the London County Council, as manager of the Royal Victoria Theatre, now the Old Vic, which stands at the northern end of the street.

Before it was named Baylis Road, the street was known as **Oakley Street**, after the oak trees that stood there originally, and there are plenty of street names in the area that recall the natural landscape, such as the self-descriptive **Upper Marsh** and **Lower Marsh** and **The Cut** (originally New Cut), which cuts a new course through the marshland. New Cut used to comprise the Upper and Lower Marsh as well, and in Victorian times the New Cut street market stretched for three miles, the longest street market in Britain. John James Sainsbury, the founder of the Sainsbury's supermarket chain, was born on Oakley Street, now Baylis Road, in 1844 and his first job was as a grocer's assistant in the New Cut market.

DISNEY STREET, SOUTHWARK, LONDON

Not actually named for film-maker Walt Disney, this street was actually named after the small village in northern France that gave its name to Walt Disney's ancestors, Isigny-sur-Mer. Members of the d'Isigny ('from Isigny') family came across to England with William the Conqueror and were given land in Lincolnshire, where they built themselves a castle and became Lords of the Manor of Norton Disney. In 1685 William Disney took the wrong side in the Monmouth Rebellion against James II and was executed, forcing the rest of the family to flee to Ireland from where they later emigrated to America - and Disney became one of the most famous names in the world. In 1949 Walt Disney himself paid a secret visit to St Peter's Church in Norton Disney to see the tombs of his ancestors. In 1965, the year before he died, he made a special trip to London to see the street named after his family and was pictured standing beneath the Disney Street sign with his wife Lillian.

ROBIN HOOD WAY, NOTTINGHAM

Celebrating Nottingham's local legend who lived in Sherwood Forest with his Merry Men and robbed the rich to give to the poor, appealing to a particularly English sense of fair play. Robin Hood, who has been brought to life on screen by numerous actors, including Richard Todd and Sean Connery, has helped to put Nottingham on the map, although not as much, perhaps, as his powerful enemy the dastardly Sheriff of Nottingham, who actually gives the city a namecheck. He is remembered in **Sheriff's Way**, while Robin Hood's love Maid Marian has **Maid Marian Way** and even the irascible Friar Tuck would be mollified to hear about his very own **Friar Lane**. Nothing, alas, for Robin Hood's giant sidekick Little John - for that you would have to travel to Nottingham, New Hampshire, in the USA, where you can find **Little John Lane**.

SPORTSMEN

BALLOON STREET, MANCHESTER

Named after the first hot-air balloon flight over Manchester that flew from here in May 1785, manned by James Sadler. In 2015 a new open space nearby was named **Sadler's Yard** in his honour, after the public were invited to suggest names for it on social media for the first time.

BLONDIN AVENUE, NORTHFIELDS, LONDON

Named after the French acrobat Charles Blondin (1824-97), famed for his tightrope walks across the Niagara Falls in America, which he completed at various times blindfolded, on stilts, wheeling a wheelbarrow, cooking and eating an omelette, carrying his manager on his back, and standing on a chair with one of its legs balanced on the rope. Blondin lived his later years in Niagara House on the road that now bears his name and died there at the age of seventy-two.

Niagara Avenue to the south recalls his Niagara exploits and the park at the end of the two streets is called Blondin Park after him.

CAPTAIN WEBB DRIVE AND WEBB CRESCENT, DAWLEY, SHROPSHIRE

Captain Matthew Webb (1848-83), the first man to swim the English Channel, is remembered here in the town where he was born. He made the swim in 1875 in less than twenty-two hours and became something of a celebrity, giving swimming lessons and performing aquatic stunts to delight the crowds. He died attempting to swim the Whirlpool Rapids below Niagara Falls.

EDWARD TEMME AVENUE, WEST HAM, LONDON

Born just down the road from his avenue, in Plaistow, Edward Temme (1904-78) was the first man to swim the English Channel both ways, from France to England in 1927 and from England to France in 1934.

SIR MATT BUSBY WAY, MANCHESTER

Previously Warwick Road North, this street runs past Manchester United's Old Trafford football ground and was renamed in honour of the club's legendary manager in 1994, the year before he died.

15

UNIQUE, UNUSUAL OR UNFORTUNATE NAMES

To finish off, here are some two hundred of the most unique, unusual or, yes, unfortunate street names from around Britain.

* **Aachen Way**, Halifax. The first street name in the alphabet, Aachen Way is named in honour of Halifax's twin city of Aachen in Germany.

* **A B Row**, Birmingham. Birmingham's shortest street is so named as it once straddled the boundary between Aston and Birmingham.

* **Adams Bottom**, Leighton Buzzard. This short lane slopes down towards a valley bottom and is named for a distinguished local family. 'Bottom' refers to a low point or valley and the term tends to appear in hillier parts of the country. When used quite innocently for a street name, the term can throw up some entertaining results, a number of which can be found in the following entries.

* **Admiral's Hard**, Plymouth. A 'hard' is a landing point and hence this is the admiral's landing place.

* **Amen Corner**, London. Amen Corner is a short street near St Paul's Cathedral. On certain feast days the clergy of St Paul's would process to the cathedral, setting off from **Paternoster Row** while chanting the Lord's Prayer in Latin, beginning with the words 'Pater noster' ('Our Father'). Amen Corner was where they would say 'Amen', having reached the end of the prayer, before going on to chant 'Hail Mary' in **Ave Maria Lane**. Nearby is **Amen Court**, a short terrace of seventeenth-century creeper-strewn houses where the canons of the cathedral live. The Campaign for Nuclear Disarmament (CND) was founded here in January 1968 in the apartment of Canon John Collins, in the presence of Labour grandees Michael Foot and Denis Healey.

* **Anchorage Terrace**, Durham. Here in medieval times an anchorite or hermit lived.

* **Anita Street**, Manchester. The name here is a corruption of 'Sanitary Street', as the Victorian terraced houses lining the road were the first in the city to have running water for lavatories and sinks.

* **Back Dykes Terrace**, Falkland, Fife. Runs along the site of the ditch or dyke that stretches around the back of the town.

* **Backside Lane**, Sibford Gower, Oxfordshire. This street name means exactly what it says, a lane at the back of the village. The same name can also be found in Doncaster and Warmsworth, South Yorkshire. There is a **Back Side** in Duggleby, North Yorkshire, which runs around the back side of the village, and a **Back Passage** by London's Smithfield Market that runs along the back of a row of buildings.

* **Bashful Alley**, Lancaster. An alley that is bashful about its past - this was once Lancaster's version of Grope Lane (see page 198), only the original name was even worse.

* **Bastard's Lane**, Great Torrington, Devon. At a stretch, I would suggest that this street name comes from the Latin *bastum*, meaning 'packsaddle', hence this lane was a way for the drivers of heavily laden horses and mules to bypass the village.

* **Beaver Close**, Hampton, Surrey. Beaver Close on the banks of the River Thames leads to the Beveree Stadium, home of Hampton and Richmond Borough FC, nicknamed the Beavers. The stadium stands in the former grounds of a house called Beveree. Beaver

Close, which was built after the stadium, could just be the result of a council official mishearing Beveree as 'beaver', although it seems likely that Beveree anyway was an alternative spelling of 'beaver', and indicates that the original house was called Beveree because it was built near a spot in the Thames where beavers lived.

* **Belcher Close**, Heather, Leicestershire. Named after the Reverend George Belcher, rector of Heather's St John the Baptist Church, who lived in Heather Manor in the mid-nineteenth century and is buried in the churchyard.

* **Bell End**, Wollaston, Northamptonshire. Innocent as I am, I had to look up why this name was considered embarrassing and I wish I hadn't. Anyway, suffice to say that Bell End is named after the Bell Inn, now closed, which stood on the corner of the street. The Bell Inn took its name from the bells of the nearby St Mary's Church. There is a Bell End in Rowley Regis in the West Midlands that recalls the bell on a hunting lodge belonging to King John that stood in the vicinity. Some residents recently petitioned to have the name changed to Bell Road but the original name remains.

* **Belland Drive**, Bristol. Named after Belland Abbey or Byland Abbey in North Yorkshire to which the Abbot of St Augustine's Abbey, now Bristol Cathedral, was appointed in the twelfth century

* **Birdcage Walk**, London. Site of King James I's aviary where the royal hunting hawks and falcons were kept.

* **Bladda Lane**, Paisley, Renfrewshire. More of a courtyard than a street, Bladda is now a car park for the Watermill Hotel built on the site of an old watermill. In Victorian times there was a fever hospital nearby, sometimes referred to as the Bladda Fever Hospital, but

it seems more likely that the hospital got its name from the street name rather than vice versa. *Bladda* is in fact an Old Scottish word for 'buttermilk', which the Victorians saw as a treatment for typhus and other infectious diseases since it contains essential minerals such as potassium and calcium. It could be that the hospital specialised in buttermilk (*bladda*) cures or that there was a dairy on the site where buttermilk (*bladda*) was made.

* **Blairmuckhole and Forestdyke Road**, Harthill, Shotts, Lanarkshire. This wonderful street name from Lanarkshire in Scotland comes close to being the longest street name in Britain (see opposite). Blairmuckhole most likely gets its name from Blairmuckhole Farm and is derived from the Scottish Gaelic words *blàr*, meaning 'cleared space', and *muc*, meaning 'pig', thus a space cleared for pigs. Forestdyke refers to a dyke or ditch on the edge of the forest. The road is actually in the middle of nowhere but passes by a clearing and an old dyke, so the name is nothing if not accurate.

* **Bleeding Heart Yard**, London. First the legend, which says that this street was named for the murder of Lady Elizabeth Hatton, daughter of Elizabeth I's Lord Chancellor Sir Christopher Hatton. She disappeared from a ball at Hatton House with the Spanish ambassador and was found next morning in the stable yard behind the house, her body torn limb from limb and her heart still pumping blood all over the cobblestones. Or it might be named after an inn called the Bleeding Heart of Our Lady, whose inn sign depicted the Virgin Mary with her heart pierced through with daggers.

* **Boghead**, Beith, Ayrshire. A doubly unfortunate name, perhaps, 'head' being the term for a ship's lavatory, which is usually found at the bow or head of a ship. Alas, Boghead is nothing more than

a description of the location of the street, at the head of a boggy patch. There are numerous Bog Lanes and Bog Roads, which likewise refer to bogs, as in wet, spongy ground.

* **Bogshole Lane**, Whitstable, Kent. Road running through a boggy hollow.

* **Bolderwood Arboretum Ornamental Drive**, New Forest. Britain's longest street name could not be more clear. This is an ornamental drive running through Bolderwood Arboretum.

* **Bootham**, York. This street runs north from Bootham Bar, York's oldest gateway (see page 49), and is named for the booths that were put up here by the monks of St Mary's Abbey for their weekly market.

* **Booty Lane**, Great Heck, North Yorkshire. 'Booty' is a corruption of the word 'butts' and indicates an area designated for archery training.

* **Bottoms Fold**, Mossley, Lancashire. There are two parts to Mossley, Top Mossley and Bottom Mosley, divided by a steep drop or 'fold' off Saddleworth Moor. Although the Bottoms Fold name quite rightly describes the street 'at the bottom of the fold', it also refers to the fold itself.

* **Brest Road**, Plymouth. Named for Plymouth's twin town of Brest, in Brittany.

* **Bull's Head Passage**, London. The name of this passage running between Leadenhall Market and Bishopsgate has two possible derivations. It could be that this was the passage along which bulls were led by the head before being slaughtered for the nearby

Leadenhall beef market. Or it could get its name from a tavern that was once in the vicinity, for there are records of a Bull Inn existing on Bishopsgate from the early sixteenth century until 1866 (see page 53). Bulls Head Passage was used for the location of the entrance to the Leaky Cauldron and Diagon Alley (see page 78) in the film *Harry Potter and the Philosopher's Stone*.

* **Busty View**, Newfield, County Durham. Street overlooking the Busty Pit coal mine that gets its name from Busty Bank, the hillside in which it is located. Apparently the hillside burst open after heavy rain to reveal the coal seam and became known as Bursty Bank and later Busty Bank.

* **Butthole Lane**, Shepshed, Leicestershire. Butts, found in most of the towns and villages of medieval England, were fields kept as practice grounds for archery - in this case an archery practice ground in a hollow. Like 'Bottom' their use in street names can lead to some unfortunate combinations. As above.

* **Butts Road**, Northampton. Also in Wellington, Somerset and Farnley Tyas, West Yorkshire. Road leading to the archery practice ground.

* **Cavalier Approach**, Leeds. Since this street runs through a modern housing estate, we must assume that it was named by an official with a devil-may-care attitude, rather than anything to do with the English Civil War.

* **Chlorine Gardens**, Belfast. Named after a nearby house called Chlorine which belonged to the nineteenth-century chemical and starch manufacturer J. W. Crawford.

* **Christmas Pie Avenue**, Normandy, Surrey. Named after a farming family called Christmas who were local landowners in the seventeenth and eighteenth centuries. The 'pie' comes from the Middle English *pightle*, meaning a small plot of land or field. In those days, fields often had names and there was one such small field owned by the Christmases that was called Pightle Field. Hence the Christmases' Pightle Field. There is one **Christmas Field**, in Sible Hedingham in Essex, a **Christmas Hill** in South Wonston in Hampshire, a **Christmas Place** in Gateshead, Tyne and Wear, and **Christmas Streets** in Liverpool and Gillingham in Kent. As all are on fairly modern housing estates, it would seem likely that they were so named because it makes the street sound nice and festive. The Christmas Street in Gillingham rather appropriately has a **Mistletoe Court**.

* **Clay Bottom**, Bristol. Road that runs along a clay valley.

* **Cock-A-Dobby**, Sandhurst. Street on the site of a former cockpit, where cockfights took place.

* **Cock Road**, Kingswood, Bristol. Named for the place where cock birds from the forest were rounded up by being driven into nets spread across the road.

* **Cockshoot Drive**, Hoveton, Norfolk. Referring to a place where woodcocks were hunted. There is also a **Cockshoot Close** in Oxfordshire and **Cockshoot Hill** in Gloucestershire.

* **Coprolite Street**, Ipswich. Coprolite is the fossilised animal dung incorporated in chemical fertilisers and found in quantity around Ipswich. This street lies on the site of a former Fisons fertiliser factory where coprolite was used.

* **Counterslip**, Bristol. A corruption of 'Countess's Slip'. A slip(way) is a smooth slope (from Middle English *slepe*) for launching a boat, and this particular slipway was constructed for an early Countess of Gloucester, possibly Isabella, daughter of the 2nd Earl of Gloucester, who became the first wife of King John. The Earls of Gloucester owned Bristol Castle.

* **Crotch Crescent**, Marston, Oxford. St Nicholas Church in Marston began life as a chapel for the monks of St Frideswide Priory in Oxford and it is entirely possible that 'Crotch' is a misspelling of 'Crutch', meaning a staff with a cross on it, as carried by the monks (see page 102). So, this street name could recall the place where monks rested with their staffs or 'crutches' as they moved between the priory and the chapel. Crescent, of course, refers to the crescent shape of the street.

* **Crumps Butts**, Bicester. Named after an archery practice ground belonging to a man called Crump.

* **Daddyhole Road**, Torquay. Road leading to Daddyhole Cove. 'Daddy' is another name for the devil, who was said to live in a cave, or hole, in the cliff facing the cove.

* **Dick Court**, Stonehouse, Lanarkshire. One can only speculate why a cul de sac of modern houses should be called Dick Court, but as all the other streets of the same housing estate seem to be named after people, we must assume that Dick was a person, most probably with a local connection. Stonehouse Online, the community website, tells us that in April 1894 a Boys' Brigade was formed in Stonehouse under the command of a Sergeant Dick. Could he be our man? He is certainly the type of local worthy who might be so honoured.

* **Dicks Mount**, Burgh St Peter, Norfolk. Dicks Mount runs along high ground above what was once the tidal estuary of the River Waveney and would have provided safe ground for ancient peoples to have lived on, especially as there is a water source called Spring Dyke at the bottom of the hill. The hill upon which Dicks Mount sits is called Devil's Stile Hill, and indeed the area is known for mysterious and unexplained happenings - due perhaps to the spirits of the prehistoric people who lived there. All of this would indicate, according to the locals, that it wasn't Dick who lived on the Mount but Old Nick, and the road was probably called Old Nick's Mount originally, then changed to something similar-sounding but less scary so as not to alarm the villagers.

* **Diversity Grove**, Perry Barr, Birmingham. One of six street names chosen from suggestions by the public for a new residential scheme that capture the 'essence of Perry Bar'. The others are **Destiny Road**, **Equality Road**, **Humanity Close**, **Inspire Avenue** and **Respect Way**.

* **Donkey Lane**, Abinger Common, Surrey. A smugglers' lane that winds and dips through Abinger village at the back of the Abinger Hatch pub. Smugglers could lead their donkeys laden with contraband along the sunken lane, hidden from view.

* **Dumb Woman's Lane**, Winchelsea, East Sussex. Named after a woman who lived on the lane and dispensed herbal remedies but who couldn't speak. There is a gruesome story of how she became mute. The lane is not far from the sea and sits in an area notorious for smuggling, and for centuries was used by smugglers bringing in illicit cargoes of lace, brandy and tobacco. One day the woman happened upon the smugglers in the lane with their contraband and had her tongue cut out so that she couldn't report the crime

to the excise men. Comedian Spike Milligan lived in a house called Carpenter's Meadow in Dumb Woman's Lane from 1988 until his death in 2002.

* **Dun Cow Lane**, Durham. The oldest named street in Durham, this short, cobbled road immediately north-east of the cathedral takes its name from the legend of the founding of Durham. The monks carrying the relics of St Cuthbert, who were searching for the legendary 'Dun Holm', or 'hill fort on an island', where they had been directed to build a church for the saint, came across a maid looking for her appropriately hued dun (greyish-brown) cow, which was last seen chewing the cud on said Dun Holm. They followed her and there built a chapel to shelter St Cuthbert's bones. The chapel became Durham Cathedral.

* **East Breast**, Greenock, Renfrewshire. East Breast is a street that can be found down by the dock in Greenock near to **East India Breast**. 'Breast' here means a low defence or parapet, as in breastwork. Hence the name refers to the east parapet of the docks, while East India Breast refers to the parapet of the East India Harbour.

* **Fanny Hands Lane**, Ludford, Lincolnshire. Named in the nineteenth century by local resident John Hands in memory of his wife Frances or 'Fanny' Hands. Apparently delivery drivers find the name Fanny funny.

* **Fanny Street**, Cardiff. Named for Frances Wood of the landowning Wood family, prominent in the nineteenth century and after whom Cardiff's **Wood Street** is named.

* **Featherbed Lane**, Shrewsbury. This street is said to be so named as it was the place where the wounded were tended after the Battle of Shrewsbury in 1403. In 2016 the name was at the centre of controversy when members of the animal rights organisation People for the Ethical Treatment of Animals (PETA) urged the council to change the name to 'Feather-free-bed Lane', since they regard using feathers in beds as cruel.

* **Feltham Close**, Romsey, Hampshire. The name Feltham comes from the Old English words *feld*, meaning 'field', and *ham*, meaning 'village', thus 'village in the field'. The original village in a field is Feltham in Middlesex, which gave its name to the de Feltham family who may have owned land in this part of Hampshire. There is another Feltham Close in Birmingham, which is most probably the site of another village in a field.

* **French Ordinary Court**, London. An 'ordinary' is, according to Dr Johnson, 'a place of eating, established at a certain price', in other words a place where every meal costs the same. There were a few such places in the City in the seventeenth and eighteenth centuries and the ordinary that stood here was established by French Huguenots for their fellow immigrants.

* **Friars Entry**, Oxford. This narrow passageway was a route from the town centre to the Franciscan friary set up beside the Thames in Oxford in the thirteenth century. Other street names that recall the friary are **Friars Wharf** and **Old Greyfriars Street**. Franciscan friars were known as Grey Friars due to the grey colour of their robes. **Roger Bacon Lane** in the same vicinity honours the thirteenth-century philosopher Roger Bacon, who studied under the Grey Friars at Oxford. The names **Paradise Square** and **Paradise Street** are a mildly ironic nod to the fact that both

Grey Friars and Black Friars had friaries in this area. Crossing the millstream at the end of Paradise Street is **Quaking Bridge**. The bridge is now made of iron but the wooden bridge that preceded it was extremely rickety and would shake or 'quake' when anyone walked across it. **Turn Again Lane**, now a street of seventeenth-century cottages set among the new Westgate Shopping Centre, was once at the centre of a web of the winding streets that made up the medieval area of St Ebbe's near the friary. The street was in modern times called Charles Street, but the old name Turn Again Lane, revived by the Oxford Preservation Society when they purchased the cottages to save them from demolition in 1971, refers to the twisting and turning nature of the lane.

* **Frying Pan Alley**, London. Named after a huge cast-iron frying pan that hung above the street to advertise an ironmonger's shop. It would regularly fall off on to the heads of passers-by and local people started to talk about that damned frying pan alley. The name stuck.

* **The Furry**, Helston, Cornwall. The Furry takes its name from Helston's annual Furry Dance, a Cornish May Day ritual that celebrates the coming of spring and dates from pagan times, one of the oldest English festivals. The word 'Furry' comes from the Cornish word *feur*, meaning 'festival'. In 1978 the Furry Dance found new fame as the subject of a hit song made popular by Sir Terry Wogan, 'The Floral Dance'.

* **Glumangate**, Chesterfield, Derbyshire. Nothing to do with UHU, this street resinates (*sic*) with music instead, as it is where, once upon a time, minstrels lived. Gluman comes from 'gleeman', an old word for a minstrel.

* **Grope Lane**, Shrewsbury. Grope Lane is where the denizens of Shrewsbury went for a grope; in other words, it was the town's red-light district. The original name for the street was considerably more explicit. There were many such lanes throughout England in the thirteenth century - most of them are now called Grape Lane (see page 38).

* **Ha Ha Road**, Woolwich. A ha ha is a sunken fence, wall or slope that provides a boundary while giving an uninterrupted view of the landscape beyond, and so this road runs along the line of an old ha ha, possibly relating to Charlton House, a Jacobean mansion half a mile to the west.

* **Happy Bottom**, Corfe Mullen, Dorset. Named after a pleasant spot located in a hollow or valley.

* **Haunch of Venison Yard**, London. This short street off Bond Street is named after the Haunch of Venison Tavern that stood at the street entrance. The tavern was named for the dish for which it was famous.

* **The Hoe**, Plymouth. Hoe means 'high ground' and Plymouth's cliff-top Hoe commands splendid views across Plymouth Sound. It was here in 1588 that Sir Francis Drake was playing bowls when the Spanish Armada sailed into view.

* **Holy Bones**, Leicester. Street leading to the graveyard of St Nicholas Church.

* **Hooker Road**, Norwich. A modern residential street, Hooker Road was named after a distinguished son of Norwich, the botanist William Jackson Hooker, who was born in the city in 1785 and

became the first director of the Royal Botanical Gardens at Kew, where he founded what has grown to be the world's largest herbarium. His son, Joseph Dalton Hooker, sailed on James Clark Ross's Antarctic expedition to the South Pole in 1839-43 - the last significant voyage of exploration made under sail alone. He also supported Charles Darwin in his research on evolution, and later succeeded his father William as director of Kew.

* **Host Street**, Bristol. A permutation of 'Horse Street' but nothing to do with horses, this street name was originally Horstrete, where 'whores' plied their trade.

* **Houndsditch**, London. Referring to the ditch where the bodies of dead dogs were deposited.

* **Ingle Pingle**, Loughborough. Named after Ingle Pingle House which stood at the end of the road. No one appears to know why you would call a house Ingle Pingle. But, then again, why not?

* **Inner Ting Tong**, Budleigh Salterton, Devon. Named after the enclosure where the Thing met, referring to the Old English word for a governing assembly (as in the Isle of Man's Tynwald) and the Old English *tun*, meaning 'enclosure'.

* **Jubbergate**, York. Originally Brettegate, the street where Celtic Britons lived, it became Jubretgate when Jews settled there, and this in turn became Jubbergate.

* **Juggs Road**, Lewes, Sussex. A 'jugg' is a basket for carrying fish and the word came to refer to those who carried such baskets, i.e. the fishermen of Brighton. Juggs Road, also known as **Juggs Lane** or **Juggs Way**, was the old road or ridgeway over the downs

along which the wives of Brighton's fishermen, or juggs, carried their freshly caught fish to the market in Lewes. There is also a **Juggs Close** in Lewes and a pub called the Juggs.

* Sometimes street names don't bother with irony but just say it as it is. There is a street near Smithfield Market that was originally called Stinking Lane because it was full of slaughterhouses. Delicate Victorian sensibilities had the name changed to **King Edward Street** instead, in honour of Edward VI who founded the Christ's Hospital for orphans nearby. Then there is Fowle Lane, which ran behind Billingsgate Fish Market by the Thames and had nothing to do with chickens, but was so called because of the foul smell of gutted fish that emanated from it. What is left of the lane is now called **Cross Street**, the name being associated with the nearby church of St Mary-at-Hill, and it ends at **Harp Lane**, named after a big house and garden, Le Harpe, that stood in the vicinity in the sixteenth century. The church gives its name to the street on which it stands, **St Mary-at-Hill**, and is so named because of it being located on the hill above Billingsgate Market.

* **Knavesmire**, York. The site today of York Racecourse, this was originally 'Knayre's Mire', which is thought to have the same derivation as Knaresborough (Chenaresburg) and means Cenheard's Mire, i.e. an area of marshland associated with someone called Cenheard.

* **The Knob**, King's Sutton, Oxfordshire. 'Knob', from the Middle Low German knobbe, meaning a protuberance or lump, usually refers to a hill or sometimes to an ancient burial place such as a hump or barrow. Since the ground around this particular Knob is completely flat, it suggests that the street must be located on the site of an ancient burial place. If you want a Knob that is indeed a hill, then

look no further than **Knob Hill** in Warnham, Sussex.

* **Ladypit Terrace**, Whitehaven, Cumbria. Named after a now defunct coal mine called the Lady Pit. Whitehaven was built on coal and was home to the first undersea coal mine, the Saltom Pit, which stretched some one and a half miles out to sea and reached a depth of 456 feet.

* **Lepper Street**, Belfast. Named after Francis Lepper, who founded a cotton manufacturing company in Belfast in 1811.

* **Letsby Avenue**, Sheffield. The name given to this quarter-mile stretch of road on an industrial estate in north-east Sheffield in the 1990s was suggested by an unlikely source - officers of the South Yorkshire police force with a sense of humour. The only building on the street? A police station.

* **Lewd Lane**, Smarden, Kent. 'Lewd' comes from the Middle English *leawde*, meaning 'unlettered, unable to read Latin' and hence 'lay', as in non-clerical, and this could be the lane in which the lay preacher lived. Many villages still have a lay preacher who is appointed to lead church services in the absence of the vicar.

* **Little Paradise**, Bristol. A street built on the site of an orchard called Little Paradise. The word 'paradise' comes from the Greek *paradeisos*, meaning 'royal enclosed park', which became a description for a heavenly place on Earth. Thus it seems likely that the orchard was considered a little heavenly place.

* **Long Lover Lane**, Halifax, West Yorkshire. Also Rimington, Lancashire. A lane where lovers would meet up, 'long' referring to the length of the lane.

* **Longbottom Avenue**, Sowerby Bridge, West Yorkshire. Road that runs along the bottom of a long valley.

* **Loonies Court**, Stockport. Since this small courtyard stands behind Stockport Town Hall, you might think it was named in honour of members of the town council, but not so. It was, in fact, named after a nineteenth-century land agent and property developer, Alexander Loonie, who had built a number of houses on the site.

* **Lower End**, Hartwell Northamptonshire. This lane runs along the lower end of the village.

* **Mangotsfield**, Bristol. Referring to Mangoda's Field, or 'field belonging to Mangoda'.

* **Mardol**, Shrewsbury. One of Shrewsbury's oldest streets, 'Mardol' means 'Devil's Boundary' and is thought to mark the boundary between the genteel part of town where the wealthy merchants lived and the town's dirty, foul-smelling tanneries.

* **Menlove Avenue**, Liverpool. Named in honour of a local draper, Alderman Thomas Menlove (1840-1913), who became chairman of the local health committee. Beatles member John Lennon lived with his aunt Mimi at Mendips, 251 Menlove Avenue, during his childhood and adolescence from 1946 to 1963.

* **Merkins Avenue**, Dumbarton. This street is named for the rateable value of the land on which it runs. A 'merk' was a silver coin, an old Scottish monetary unit, and 'merkin' denotes a piece of land worth one mark, i.e. a 'merkland' or 'merkin'.

* **Mincing Lane**, London. Nothing to do with chopping things up very small or walking in a certain way, Mincing Lane takes its name from the 'mynchens' or nuns of the nearby church of St Helen's Bishopsgate who had their dwellings here. The word comes from the Anglo-Saxon *minicen* or *minchery*, meaning 'nun' and 'nunnery' respectively. The name of the Cotswold town of Minchinhampton in Gloucestershire derives from *minicen*, too. In the nineteenth century, Mincing Lane was the world's hub for tea trading and, before that, the centre of the opium trade. As Charles Dickens writes in *Our Mutual Friend*: '[Bella] arrived in the drug-flavoured region of Mincing Lane, with the sensation of having just opened a drawer in a chemist's shop.'

* **Minge Lane**, Upton upon Severn, Worcestershire. An embarrassing name - but not in the way you might think if you were born after 1903, when 'minge' acquired a more unfortunate meaning. Before that, 'minge' was an old word for 'to urinate', and since Minge Lane was used by animals being taken to graze on the village common, the name no doubt refers to what the animals got up to as they passed along the lane.

* **Moat**, Castle Donington, Leicestershire. The clue is in the name of the village - this street is on the site of the old castle moat.

* **Mount Pleasant**, Clerkenwell, London. This street gives its name to what was once the world's largest postal sorting office, Mount Pleasant, built on the site of Britain's largest prison, the infamous Cold Bath Fields Prison, described in the poem 'The Devil's Thoughts' by Samuel Taylor Coleridge and Robert Southey:

> *As he went through the Cold-Bath Fields he saw*
> *A solitary cell;*

And the devil was pleased, for it gave him a hint
For improving his prisons in Hell.

The name 'Cold Baths' recalls the medicinal cold baths that were located here in the seventeenth century. The street name Mount Pleasant is ironic and was applied in the eighteenth century to a country lane that led down the hill to the River Fleet and became a place for dumping refuse and rubbish. The name of **Laystall Street**, which runs off Mount Pleasant, indicates there was a laystall or holding area for cattle going to market here, and the accumulated dung and mess associated with this would have attracted further waste and litter.

* **No Name Street**, Sandwich, Kent. This street that links two main streets is so short that the doors of the buildings on it open on to the two streets it joins, meaning it wasn't necessary to name the street as part of an address and hence it was left with no name. Except, of course, the name 'No Name Street'.

* **Nork Rise**, Banstead, Surrey. Apparently 'nork' is Australian slang for 'breast', hence the comic connotations of this street name. **Nork Rise**, **Nork Gardens**, **Nork Way** and **Nork Park** can all be found in Nork, a south London suburb near Banstead. Nork is named after Nork House, now demolished, built here in 1740 by Sir Christopher Buckle, who is remembered by **Buckles Way**. The name Nork is derived from the Latin *noverca*, meaning 'stepmother', but commonly used by Roman soldiers to describe a dominating feature such as a hill or a wood that overlooks and thus weakens a military camp, providing a strategic advantage for an enemy. Nork House stood on a hill overlooking a former Roman camp, hence the name, which originally applied to the field on which the house was built.

* **Ogleforth**, York. The name is thought to be Old Norse for a ford where an owl lived.

* **Old Sodom Lane**, Dauntsey, Wiltshire. Sodom is not, alas, named after the biblical city consumed by fire and brimstone for the sins of its inhabitants. It is, instead, another word for 'sodden' and refers to an area constantly underwater or marshy. Dauntsey comes from the Saxon *Dantes-eig*, meaning 'Dante's island', and sits on high ground above the floodplain of the River Avon. **Sodom Lane** and Old Sodom Lane lead from Dauntsey to an area down in the floodplain known as Sodom, as in 'sodden'. There is also a Sodom Lane in Marnhull in Dorset, which leads down to the floodplain of the River Stour above which the village sits on a low ridge. There is a village called **Sodom** on the Shetland Isle of Whalsay whose name is a corruption of the Old Norse *sudheim*, meaning 'south home'.

* **Oscar Road**, Aberdeen. Named after a whaling ship called *Oscar* which was driven ashore in Greyhope Bay off Aberdeen in 1813, with the loss of forty-two lives.

* **Pant-y-Felin Road**, Pontarddulais, Swansea. A simple one: according to its name, this road runs along the valley of the mill. *Pant* is Welsh for 'valley' or 'hollow', while *y* means 'the' and *felin* means 'mill'.

* **Pasture Rise**, Bridlington. Slightly rising street in a modern housing estate built on pasture land.

* **Pavement**, York. The site of York's earliest market, this street was first known as Marketshire but in the early fourteenth century it was one of the first streets in York since Roman times to be paved, and hence became known as Pavement.

* **Peep-O-Day Lane**, Abingdon, Oxfordshire. This quiet country lane on the southern edge of Abingdon runs along the side of the Thames river meadows, and is so named because it offers a clear view across the river of the sun rising at daybreak. The **Peep O'Day Lane** in Dundee, running through an industrial area, was named after a house belonging to the Ogilvy family (Earls of Airlie) that stood on the site until the end of the nineteenth century. It was called Peep O'Day Mansion as it faced east towards the dawn.

* **Pennycomequick Hill**, Plymouth. Takes its name from the area. *Pen* is a Brittonic Celtic word for 'head', *y* is 'the', *cwm* is 'valley' and *krik* is creek, hence 'valley at the head of the creek'. Simple.

* **Percy Passage**, London. Like the adjoining **Percy Street** and **Percy Mews**, Percy Passage took its name from the Percy Coffee House, which stood on the corner of Rathbone Place. It was a haunt of writers, including Dr Johnson's biographer James Boswell, and in 1820 two of them, writing under the pen names Reuben and Sholto Percy, published the hugely popular *Percy Anecdotes*, a collection of stories they picked up in the coffee house.

* **The Peth**, Alnwick, Northumberland. A *peth* is a street that descends down to a river and The Peth in Alnwick does exactly that, leading down to the Lion Bridge over the River Aln, named for the lion emblem of the Percy family.

* **Piccadilly**, London. In 1612 Robert Baker, who had a tailor's shop on the Strand, built himself a country house on land north of what is now Piccadilly Circus. Since his wealth came from the sale of 'picadils', a type of broad, starched lace collar fashionable in the sixteenth and seventeenth centuries, the house was nicknamed Piccadilly Hall, and over time the street on which

the house stood, originally called Portugal Street in honour of Charles II's Portuguese queen, Catherine of Braganza, became known as Piccadilly.

* **Pink Lane**, Newcastle upon Tyne. Named for the Pink Tower, one of the seventeen towers that guarded Newcastle's thirteenth-century town walls. Rather than reflecting the colour of its walls, the name probably comes from the Dutch word *pink*, meaning, essentially, 'little finger', but also used to mean 'small' or 'narrow'. Hence 'small tower', perhaps in relation to the other, larger, towers in the same way as a little finger is to the other fingers.

* **Pitch and Pay Lane**, Stoke Bishop, Bristol. There is a legend that Pitch and Pay Lane refers to times of plague, when country folk would bring food to the plague-ridden city and pitch it across the road in return for payment in coins that were pitched back. In fact it was named after the seventeenth-century Pitch and Pay House, home of Sir Robert Cann, master of the Merchant Venturers, who was infamous for not allowing credit. 'Pitch and pay' was an old expression meaning to pay at the time of purchase, which is what Sir Robert demanded from his tenants who would go to the house to 'pitch and pay'. Another Bristol expression meaning 'to pay on time' is 'pay on the nail', which comes from the custom whereby merchants would pay for goods by placing their money on flat-topped brass columns called 'nails' that stand in the street outside Bristol's Corn Exchange.

* **Pump Alley**, Bolton Percy, North Yorkshire. This Pump Alley and all the other lanes and streets and roads that bear the name 'pump' are named after pumps, usually for pumping water.

* **Quality Street**, Davidson's Mains, Edinburgh. Named, like the chocolates, after the eponymous play by J. M. Barrie, author of

Peter Pan. Barrie himself had taken the name from Quality Street in Leith, which was so named to reflect Leith's reputation as a port. In 1967 the Leith Quality Street was renamed Maritime Street to avoid confusion with the Quality Street in Davidson's Main, even though the latter was named a long time after the Leith street.

* **Ramsbottom Lane**, Ramsbottom, Bury, Lancashire. The good old Yorkshire name of Ramsbottom comes from the Old English words *hramsa*, meaning 'wild garlic' (and hence 'ramsons'), and *botm*, meaning 'valley', thus 'valley of the wild garlic'. The early Ramsbottoms were thus the people who lived in the valley of the wild garlic.

* **Rye**, Puriton, Somerset. The shortest street name in Britain, Rye most probably comes from the Old English word *rie* or *rhee*, meaning 'bank of a river'. Puriton lies in the marshy low-lying Sedgemoor area of ditches and dykes, and Rye is a very ancient curving street that looks as if it follows the course of a former river or stream.

* **Salmon Lane**, Limehouse, London. Not named for the King of Fish but rather for the nearest church, St Dunstan's, in Stepney. 'Salmon' is a common corruption of the word 'sermon' and this was the road people had to take to church to hear one.

* **Shoulder of Mutton Alley**, Limehouse, London. Now lined with smart apartment blocks, this short street takes its name from the Shoulder of Mutton Tavern that stood here. The tavern got its name in turn from a nearby meat market. The original *Spitting Image* puppets were made in a workshop in the street.

* **Slack Bottom**, Hebden Bridge, West Yorkshire. This street lies at the bottom of Slack Hill and is named after the tiny hamlet of Slack,

whose name in turn comes from the Middle English *slack*, which has several meanings, including 'loose' or 'surplus', as in the slack of a rope, or 'small pieces'. Since there were coal mines nearby, the slack referred to is most likely coal slack, i.e. coal dust or small pieces of coal (that are surplus to requirements). The top of Slack Hill is called, astonishingly, **Slack Top**.

* **Slag Lane**, Westbury, Wiltshire. In the 1840s iron ore was discovered just north of Westbury and an ironworks was established to exploit the find. The workings produced slag heaps made up of the material left over once the iron ore had been extracted. After the ironworks closed, the slag heaps were reclaimed and Slag Lane was built on the site. There is also a Slag Lane in Haydock on Merseyside, site of a former ironworks, and another in Pontesford in Shropshire and in Golborne near Wigan, both former coal-mining communities, coal mining producing its own kind of slag heap.

* **Slutshole Lane**, Beeston, Norfolk. Formerly Slutch Hole Lane, meaning 'muddy hollow lane', from the archaic 'slutch', meaning 'mud', and 'hole' as in 'hollow'.

* **Smellies Lane**, Dundee. Smellie, pronounced 'Smiley', is an ancient and distinguished Scottish name, and this lane is most probably named for a member of the Smellie family.

* **Snatchup**, Redbourne, Hertfordshire. This street is in an area that used to be called Snatchup End, and this is thought to be where the stagecoach would 'snatch up' the mail bags as it passed.

* **Spanker Lane**, Nether Heage, Derbyshire. Spanker Lane leads to the Spanker pub from which it takes its name. A 'spanker' is

an old-fashioned term for a fast horse, and as the story goes, a previous landlord changed the name of the pub to that of his racehorse, Spanker, to celebrate the horse winning a valuable race.

* **Squeeze-ee-Belly Alley**, Port Isaac, Cornwall. This alley, thought to be the narrowest thoroughfare in England, was originally named Temple Bar, but since it is impossible to pass through without breathing in, difficult after a Cornish cream tea, it became known by its rather more descriptive nickname and eventually the name stuck. There is also a **Squeezebelly Lane**, all one word and with just one 'e', in Kingsbridge, next door in Devon, a county also rich in cream teas.

* **Squeeze Guts Alley**, Truro, Cornwall. Another narrow Cornish alley where you have to breathe in.

* **Staines Road**, Feltham, London. The road to Staines, whose name comes from the Old English *stan*, meaning 'stone'. Staines is the site of the London Stone placed next to the River Thames in 1285 to mark the western limit of the Corporation of London's jurisdiction over the river.

* **Stalkers Entry**, Blackford, Perthshire. The word 'stalker' comes from the Gaelic *stalcaire*, which means a hunter or falconer, and so this short street is likely to have been the way by which hunters or falconers set forth or returned from the nearby Ochil Hills. Blackford is home to Highland Spring, Britain's bestselling mineral water, which is sourced from the Ochils.

* **The Street With No Name**, Teignmouth, Devon. A misleading name, of course, because the name of the street - like No Name Street on page 205 - is The Street With No Name, but the reason behind the

strange name is that this was not a planned street but is simply a gap between houses that emerged when the area was redeveloped.

* **Swallow Street**, London. Swallow Street used to run straight from St James's to Oxford Street but most of it was demolished to make way for Regent Street. **Swallow Passage**, which becomes **Swallow Place**, is what is left of the northern part of Swallow Street where it meets Oxford Street. A short section of Swallow Street survives at the southern end, near Piccadilly Circus. Swallow Street began life in the sixteenth century as Swallow Close, taking its name from the first tenant, Thomas Swallow.

* **There and Back Again Lane**, Bristol. There is no certain origin to this unique street name. It is a short cul de sac and it is possible that the name refers to the fact that once you go down it, you have to come back again. Or it could have been inspired by the alternative title of J. R. R. Tolkien's *The Hobbit*, which is *There and Back Again*.

* **Tickle Cock Bridge**, Castleford, West Yorkshire. When this pedestrian passageway was built under the railway lines in 1890, it quickly became a place where the young people of the neighbourhood would go for a bit of fun - hence the name. When it was rebuilt in 2008 the council changed the name to Tittle Cott, but a campaign was launched by the local residents to have the old name restored.

* **Titty Ho**, Raunds, Northamptonshire. No one seems to know where this street name comes from, although many have come up with suggestions. 'Ho' is most probably short for 'House', but 'Titty' is unclear. A place where birds such as blue tits gather, some say, others that there must have been a family called Titty living here.

My own best guess is that Titty is a corruption of 'Tithe', as in the tithes paid to the church in times gone by, when every working person had to donate one-tenth of their income or produce to their local church. The produce was stored in a tithe barn or, in this case, a tithe house, suggesting that Titty Ho occupies the site of the old village tithe house. Of course, it could just be someone on the council with a sense of humour or an eye to publicity . . .

* **Tom Tit Lane**, Woodham Mortimer, Essex. I remember getting great pleasure from the name of a wood called Tomtits Bottom near my childhood home in Gloucestershire. My geography teacher informed me that Tom Tit was a colloquial name for a common bird such as blue tit or great tit, and the wood was therefore a 'wood full of birds at the bottom of a slope or hill', which indeed it is. On that basis, Tom Tit Lane would be a lane full of birds and since it is a pleasant country lane, this is entirely plausible.

* **Tooley Street**, London. Referring to St Olave's Church, which stood at the end of the street. The name was gradually corrupted to St Toulus, St Toolis and finally St Toolies. St Olave was in reality Olaf Haraldsson, the future King of Norway who, to help Ethelred the Unready retake London from Canute, tied his boats to London Bridge and pulled it down, thus giving us the nursery rhyme 'London Bridge is Falling Down'.

* **Toot Hill Butts**, Headington. On the site of a field called Toot Hill that was kept for archery practice. 'Toot' comes from the Germanic *tuten*, meaning 'to blow a horn', so this area was probably used for hunting.

* **Trump Street**, London. Trump Street was not named for a controversial US president but rather because it was the street

where trumpet makers plied their trade, 'trump' being an old-fashioned term for a trumpet.

* **Turnagain Lane**, Canterbury. Once you have reached the end of this cul de sac, you must turn again and go back, rather as in There and Back Again Lane on page 212.

* **Ugly Lane**, Nettlesworth, County Durham. Ugly Lane is in fact a rather pretty residential lane that becomes a farm track, and is located on the edge of the small mining village of Nettlesworth. It runs past a school, which is perhaps why there is no road sign - to avoid the obvious youthful hilarity. There is a village in Essex called Ugley whose name is said to mean 'Ugga's clearing', from the name Ugga and the Old English *leah*, 'clearing in a wood', so we can perhaps surmise that Ugly Lane means the same - a clearing in the wood where Ugga lived.

* **Upper Butts**, Brentford. Named after the upper archery practice ground.

* **Uranus Road**, Hemel Hempstead. Part of a development of houses nicknamed the Planets, in which all of the roads are named after planets or other celestial objects: **Jupiter Drive**, **Neptune Drive**, **Apollo Way**, **Pluto Rise**, **Saturn Way**, **Mercury Walk** and **Martian Avenue**.

* **Vulcan Street**, Aberystwyth. Named after the Roman god of fire, in reference to a smithy that stood on the street.

* **Welsh Back**, Bristol. Here the buildings 'back' on to the docks where Welsh ships used to moor up.

* **Wham Bottom Lane**, Rochdale, Lancashire. 'Wham' comes from the Old Norse *hvammr*, meaning 'grassy slope', and this small lane does indeed lie at the bottom of a grassy slope, although the first house in the lane perhaps describes the situation in a less impenetrable way - Spring Bank Cottage.

* **Whip-Ma-Whop-Ma-Gate**, York. The shortest street in York with the longest name. It is first mentioned in 1505, when it was known as Whitnourwhatnourgate and later Whitney Whatneygate. This can either be translated from the Middle English as 'what a street', as in 'what a surprising street this is', or, because the street looks as much like a square as a street, as 'neither one thing nor the other'.

* **Willey Lane**, Nottingham. The lane of willow trees, from the Anglo-Saxon word *wilig*, meaning willow.

* **Wine Street**, Bristol. Not the place where wine was traded but a permutation of the original name, Wynch Street, which according to one suggestion was named after a winch that operated a pillory or stocks that stood in the middle of the street. The name is a good example of regional etymology, 'Wine Street' as a derivation of 'Wynch Street' being found only in those parts of the south-west and South Wales that traded with each other. Another suggestion is that Wynch came from the Middle English *winche*, meaning a water pit or well - the street conjoins with **The Pithay**, also named after a deep water pit or well.

* **Winkle Street**, Liverpool. A winkle is a shore-dwelling mollusc. There are also Winkle Streets in Southampton and on the Isle of Wight (Calbourne), all close to the seashore and undoubtedly where winkles were processed and sold. However, the exception that proves the rule is Winkle Street in West Bromwich in the Black

Country, which couldn't be further from the sea, but as this Winkle Street is on an industrial estate, I can only assume that it was once the site of a seafood-processing business. Winkles are often paired with cockles, as in cockles and winkles, and there is a **Cockles Lane** in Weymouth, indicating that cockles were sold there.

* **Wolfhill Road**, Belfast. Skirts the hill where the last wolf in the Belfast area was killed.

* **Worship Street**, Shoreditch, London. Shoreditch was once known for its cloth workers and tailors, and Worship Street is probably named after one of them, a seventeenth-century tailor called Worsop who lived and worked on the street.

* **Zurich Gardens**, Bramhall, Stockport. The last street name in the alphabet, and one of a cluster of streets in Bramhall in an area known as Little Switzerland, where the streets are named after Swiss cities: **Basle Close**, **Berne Close**, **Geneva Road**, **Lausanne Road**, **Lucerne Road** and **Lugano Road**.

INDEX OF PLACENAMES

The Ocean at the End of the
Lane, Portsmouth 178
Winston Churchill Avenue,
Portsmouth 127

Herefordshire
Drapers Lane, Leominster 93

Hertfordshire
Apollo Way, Hemel
Hempstead 214
Easy Way, Luton 9
Jupiter Drive, Hemel
Hempstead 214
Little Bushey Lane, Bushey 69
Martian Avenue, Hemel
Hempstead 214
Mercury Walk, Hemel
Hempstead 214
Neptune Drive, Hemel
Hempstead 214
Pluto Rise, Hemel Hempstead
214
Saturn Way, Hemel
Hempstead 214
Snatchup, Redbourne 210
Spicer Street, St Albans 94
Stationers Place, Hemel
Hempstead 97-98
Uranus Road, Hemel
Hempstead 214

Kent
Bogshole Lane, Whitstable 191
Butchery Lane, Canterbury 95
Christmas Street, Gillingham
193
Fort Road, Broadstairs 176
King Lear's Way, Dover 130
Lewd Lane, Smarden 202
Mistletoe Court, Gillingham
193
No Name Street, Sandwich
205
Queen Bertha's Avenue,
Margate 131

Queen Bertha Road,
Ramsgate 131
Queen Elizabeth II Bridge,
Dartford 131
Quenin Gate, Canterbury 51
Red House Lane, Bexleyheath
107
Turnagain Lane, Canterbury
214
Wincheap, Canterbury 95

Lancashire
Bashful Alley, Lancaster 188
Bottoms Fold, Mossley 191
James Towers Way, Preston
123-124
Ramsbottom Lane, Bury 209
Sustainability Way, Leyland 62
Wham Bottom Lane, Rochdale
215

Leicester
Alma Street 159
Beatrice Road 159
Hawthorne Street 159
Holy Bones 199
Ivanhoe Street 160
Newport Street 160
Oban Street 160
Rowan Street 159
Ruby Street 159-160
Sylvan Street 160

Leicestershire
Belcher Close, Heather 189
Butthole Lane, Shepshed 192
Ingle Pingle, Loughborough
200
Moat, Castle Donington 204

Lincolnshire
Castle Square, Lincoln 80
Fanny Hands Lane, Ludford
196
Isaac Newton Way, Grantham
171

Steep Hill, Lincoln 80
The Strait, Lincoln 80
Well Lane, Lincoln 113

Liverpool
Albany Road 137
Albert Edward Road 136
Apple Court 180
Beaconsfield Street 125
Brunswick Road 137
Canning Street 125
Cavern Court 180
Christmas Street 193
Connaught Road 137
David Street 104
Empress Road 136
George Harrison Close 180
Gladstone Avenue/Road/
Street 125
Huskisson Street 125
Isaac Street 104
Jacob Street 104
John Lennon Drive 62, 180
Jubilee Drive 136
Leopold Road 137
Menlove Avenue 203
Moses Street 104
Paul McCartney Way 180
Penny Lane 19
Ringo Starr Drive 180
Salisbury Road 125-126
Scotland Road 85
Sir Thomas Street 172
Winkle Street 215-216

London
Abbey Road 102
Addison Avenue/Crescent/
Gardens/Place 175
Addison Road 175
Addle Hill 91
Albert Embankment 129
Albert Square 143
Aldersgate 52
Aldgate 53
Amen Corner/Court 187

Marne Crescent, Rochdale 124
Mons Avenue, Rochdale 124
Mosley Street 155
Palatine Road, Withington 84
Quay Street 112
Radium Street 168
Salford Quays 29
Shambles Square 96
Simonsway 168-169
Sir Matt Busby Way 185
Tib Lane/Street 74
Verdun Crescent, Rochdale
  124
Whitworth Street 169
Zurich Gardens, Bramhall,
  Stockport 5, 216

Merseyside
Lord Street, Southport 16
Victoria Road, Formby 129

Newcastle upon Tyne
Blackett Street 169
Bolingbroke Street 178
Clayton Street 169
Collingwood Street 119
Cox Chare 40
John Dobson Street 169
Fenkle Street 78
Grainger Street 162
Grey Street 124-125
Hood Street 169
Hotspur Street 178
Malcolm Street 178
Mosley Street 170
Mowbray Street 178
Neville Street 155-156
Nun Street 104
Percy Street 156
Pilgrim Street 13
Pink Lane 208
Pitt Street 127
Pudding Chare 40
Shakespeare Street 179
Stowell Street 169
Stratford Road 178

Strawberry Lane/Place 104
Trinity Chare 40
Warwick Street 178
Worswick Street 169

Norfolk
Cockshoot Drive, Hoveton
  193
Dicks Mount, Burgh St Peter
  195
Elizabeth Fry Road, Norwich
  124
Elm Hill, Norwich 66-67
Geoffrey Road, Norwich
  170-171
Hooker Road, Norwich
  199-200
Opie Street, Norwich 126
Saturday Market Place, King's
  Lynn 94
Slutshole Lane, Beeston 210
South Quay, Great Yarmouth
  29
Tuesday Market Place, King's
  Lynn 94

Northamptonshire
Bell End, Wollaston 189
Butts Road, Northampton 192
Lower End, Hartwell 203
Titty Ho, Raunds 212-213

Northumberland
Bailiffgate, Alnwick 47
Bondgate Within, Alnwick 47
Bondgate Without, Alnwick
  47
Copper Chare, Morpeth 40
Fenkle Street, Alnwick 78
Narrowgate, Alnwick 47
Pottergate, Alnwick 47
The Peth, Alnwick 207
Walkergate, Alnwick 48

Nottingham
Carrington Street 170

Castle Boulevard 16
Friar Lane 184
Gregory Boulevard 16
Isandula Road 122
Jesse Boot Avenue 170
Lenton Boulevard 16
Lister Gate 93
Lucknow Avenue 122
Maid Marian Way 184
Nelson Street 122
Nile Street 122
Radford Boulevard 16
Robin Hood Way 184
Sheriff's Way 184
Trafalgar Street 122
University Boulevard 16
Willey Lane 215
Zulu Road 122

Nottinghamshire
Station Road, Scrooby 15

Oxfordshire
Backside Lane, Sibford Gower
  188
Beef Lane, Oxford 96
Butchers Row, Banbury 95
Carfax, Oxford 116
Cockshoot Close, Stonesfield
  193
Crotch Crescent, Marston 194
Crumps Butts, Bicester 194
Crutch Furlong, Berinsfield
  103
Friars Entry, Oxford 197-198
Friars Wharf, Oxford 197
Old Greyfriars Street, Oxford
  197
Paradise Square/Street,
  Oxford 197
Peep-O-Day Lane, Abingdon
  207
Quaking Bridge, Oxford 198
Roger Bacon Lane, Oxford 197
The Knob, King's Sutton
  201-202

NORTHERN IRELAND

Belfast

Agincourt Avenue/Street 120
Cairo Street 104
Carmel Street 104
Castle Arcade 40
Castle Place/Street 111
Cave Hill 111
Chlorine Gardens 192
Crown Entry 40
Crumlin Road 78

Damascus Street 104
Jerusalem Street 104
Joy's Entry 40
Lepper Street 202
Ormeau Road 106
Palestine Street 104
Pottinger's Entry 40
Prince Edward Drive 132
Shankill Road 105
Sugar House Entry 41
Winecellar Entry 41
Wolfhill Road 216
Wolseley Street 172

ACKNOWLEDGEMENTS

My thanks to the home team at Quadrille for all their splendid work in helping to put this book together: to the design team for making the book look so good, to Sofie Shearman for her guidance and professionalism in pulling the book together and to Kate Parker for her expert and sympathetic editing.

Special thanks to my publishing director Sarah Lavelle, without whose inspiration and support this book would never have happened.

SOURCES

Local newspaper, local authority and local museum archives have been the most helpful sources of information for compiling this book, as have the following two websites:

streetlist.co.uk The A-Z of Street Names in the United Kingdom
laputa.it/street-types Toponymy: Street Types